Karate

A Comprehensive Guide to Karate Techniques for Beginners Wanting to Go from Basics to Black Belt

© Copyright 2024 - All rights reserved.

The content contained within this book may not be reproduced, duplicated, or transmitted without direct written permission from the author or the publisher.

Under no circumstances will any blame or legal responsibility be held against the publisher, or author, for any damages, reparation, or monetary loss due to the information contained within this book, either directly or indirectly.

Legal Notice:

This book is copyright protected. It is only for personal use. You cannot amend, distribute, sell, use, quote or paraphrase any part of the content within this book, without the consent of the author or publisher.

Disclaimer Notice:

Please note the information contained within this document is for educational and entertainment purposes only. All effort has been executed to present accurate, up-to-date, reliable, and complete information. No warranties of any kind are declared or implied. Readers acknowledge that the author is not engaging in the rendering of legal, financial, medical, or professional advice. The content within this book has been derived from various sources. Please consult a licensed professional before attempting any techniques outlined in this book.

By reading this document, the reader agrees that under no circumstances is the author responsible for any losses, direct or indirect, that are incurred as a result of the use of the information contained within this document, including, but not limited to, errors, omissions, or inaccuracies.

Table of Contents

INTRODUCTION 1
CHAPTER 1: THE KARATE MINDSET 3
CHAPTER 2: KIHON I STANCES AND BLOCKS 13
CHAPTER 3: KIHON II PUNCHES AND KICKS 26
CHAPTER 4: WHITE AND YELLOW BELT KATAS AND KUMITE 38
CHAPTER 5: ORANGE AND GREEN BELT KATAS AND KUMITE 49
CHAPTER 6: PURPLE AND BROWN BELT KATAS 60
CHAPTER 7: BROWN AND BLACK BELT KUMITES 74
CHAPTER 8: BLACK BELT KATAS I 81
CHAPTER 9: BLACK BELT KATAS II 93
CHAPTER 10: UNDERSTANDING BELTS AND THE DOJO 103
CHAPTER 11: HOW TO DEFEND YOURSELF WITH KARATE 113
CHAPTER 12: DAILY TRAINING DRILLS 120
EXTRA: PRESSURE POINTS OVERVIEW AND KARATE TERMS 124
CONCLUSION 128
HERE'S ANOTHER BOOK BY CLINT SHARP THAT YOU MIGHT LIKE 130
REFERENCES 131

Introduction

Have you ever wondered what it is like to be a student of karate? Have you always wanted to learn an ancient and powerful martial art but don't know where to begin? This book gives you all the information to get started and master this timeless art.

Karate focuses on enhancing the mind, body, and spirit. It's about striking and kicking and building character, discipline, and resilience. With each technique and form, you'll learn to focus your mind, harness your strength, and push your limits. You'll move through the ranks quickly when you practice karate diligently as your skills and understanding grow.

The dedication and commitment instilled in karate practitioners go far beyond the dojo walls and affect every aspect of their lives. Developing a karate mindset requires mental toughness, an unbreakable will, and a never-give-up attitude. With these traits, a karateka can overcome physical challenges and obstacles they face in life. Karate's fundamental principles and training methods are the foundation for any practitioner, regardless of belt rank. Properly understanding stances, blocks, punches, kicks, katas, and kumite is essential for a successful martial arts journey.

Karate belts are not just a piece of cloth tied around a martial artist's waist. They represent milestones and achievements in their karate journey. Each belt color has significance and symbolizes the hard work and dedication of the karateka. From the beginner's white belt to the experienced black belt, the journey is a never-ending process of learning and improving. The karate community is excited and proud when a karateka enters the dojo wearing a new belt. Each belt color is meaningful and vital to the karateka's journey. It brings a sense of accomplishment and proves that pushing yourself to the limit is worth it.

This comprehensive guide dives into the details of karate, from stances and blocks to katas and kumite. You'll discover the basics, advanced techniques, pressure points, and drills. You gain insight into karate culture and what it takes to master this martial art. From the importance of respect to the power of the karate mindset, this book teaches you everything about this ancient art.

Before you begin your journey, arm yourself with knowledge. Read this book and learn the information needed to succeed as a karateka. With the right mindset and dedication, you can defend yourself and impress your friends with impressive forms and techniques. So, get ready to experience the power of karate and take your martial arts journey to the next level.

Chapter 1: The Karate Mindset

Are you ready to master physical and mental prowess? Can you restructure your mindset and develop an unshakable spirit? Karate enhances your physical strength and agility and teaches you the value of self-confidence and discipline.

The karate mindset focuses on training your mind to be as strong as your body.
https://unsplash.com/photos/UpFy6jbnXS4?utm_source=unsplash&utm_medium=referral&utm_content=creditShareLink

The karate mindset is about training your mind to be as strong as your body. It's about pushing beyond your limits and tapping into a level of focus and discipline you never thought possible. Adopting the karate mindset, you become more patient, humble, and resilient. You learn to embrace failure as a steppingstone to success and develop a deep appreciation for the power of hard work and perseverance.

Whether a seasoned martial artist or a complete beginner, this chapter helps you understand karate's philosophical teachings and psychological aspects passed down for centuries. It briefly overviews the four main karate styles, their corresponding techniques, and the three main elements of karate in detail. Mastering these concepts will take your physical and mental skills to the next level.

Philosophical Teachings of Karate

To truly understand karate, you must delve deep and embrace its philosophical teachings. Karate has taught individuals to help them to become more self-aware, find inner peace, and develop discipline beyond the dojo. Understanding the philosophical teachings of karate is essential for unlocking the full potential and true essence of this ancient art. This section explores the connection between mind and body harmony in traditional karate teachings.

Awareness

One of the fundamental teachings of karate is awareness. karate practitioners are always taught to be present in the moment, aware of their surroundings, and alert to potential danger. This awareness is essential in self-defense and daily life. Knowing your surroundings, actions, and thoughts can help you navigate life with better clarity and avoid unnecessary distractions. The heightened awareness that comes with being a karate practitioner is a powerful tool for self-improvement and personal growth.

Mind and Body Unity

Karate teaches that the mind and body are not separate entities but interconnected. Practicing karate, you learn to master your mind and body, aligning them with each other. You know to use your mind to control your body and your body to support your mind. As a result, karate training enhances mental clarity and concentration, increases physical strength and flexibility, and improves overall health and well-being. By practicing karate, you develop a deeper connection between your mind and body – which is essential to achieving your goals and finding inner peace.

Discipline

Another critical teaching in karate is discipline. Karate requires discipline in everything you do, from training and practicing to daily life. Discipline is what separates a martial artist from a mere fighter. Martial artists are disciplined individuals dedicated to pursuing excellence in all aspects of life. You learn to respect yourself, others, and the world around you through discipline. Disciplined individuals can focus their attention and energy on achieving their goals without being distracted by negative thoughts or external influences.

Humility

Humility is a cornerstone of traditional karate teaching. Humility is recognizing your limitations, weaknesses, strengths, and abilities. Karate teaches that everyone should approach training with an open mind and a willingness to learn from others, regardless of skill or rank. Embracing humility, you see yourself and others as equal, developing tolerance and respect. Humility prevents arrogance and ego, which can significantly hinder personal growth.

Perseverance

Perseverance is the ability to persist in the face of adversity and to stay committed to your goals despite challenges and setbacks. Karate training can be physically and mentally demanding, requiring much perseverance to progress in skill and rank. Perseverance is essential in developing a strong spirit, crucial for overcoming obstacles and achieving success. By creating a resilient and determined mindset, you can overcome any challenge.

The philosophical teachings of karate are essential for unlocking the full potential of this ancient art. The teachings of awareness, mind and body unity, discipline, humility, and perseverance all contribute to a holistic approach to life. The ultimate goal of karate is not only to become physically strong or skilled in martial techniques but also to become a better human and live a more fulfilling life. A better insight into karate's more profound meaning and purpose can help you achieve mind and body harmony.

Importance of Right Kokoro

Karate is a physical sport and a mental discipline that requires a balanced blend of mind and body. Therefore, the Kokoro, the Japanese term for heart, mind, and spirit, is vital in the practice of karate. Your kokoro should be pure and focused, allowing you to concentrate on the task and perform it to your fullest potential. This section discusses why having the right kokoro is crucial in karate and how it impacts your overall performance.

A Strong Kokoro Helps You Overcome Challenges

A strong kokoro means having a clear focus and a positive mindset. When you practice karate, there will be times when you encounter challenges seemingly impossible to overcome. However, having the right kokoro enables you to push through these challenges with grit, determination, and a never-say-die attitude. It helps you keep your composure in adversity and makes you a better, more resilient karate practitioner.

A Clear Kokoro Helps You Develop Your Technique

The importance of the right kokoro in karate goes beyond mental fortitude. A clear mind helps you learn and master techniques effectively. When mentally distracted, your body will naturally follow, resulting in incorrect posture and movement. Conversely, when your kokoro is clear and focused, your actions become more precise, and your activities become more fluid. You will develop your technique faster and achieve better results on the mat.

A Pure Kokoro Helps You Connect with Your Training Partners

Having the right kokoro allows you to connect with your training partners deeper. When your heart is pure, your energy is positive, and your intentions are sincere. It creates an environment of mutual respect and trust, fostering an excellent training atmosphere where everyone can grow and learn together.

An Inclusive Kokoro Helps You Promote Unity and Camaraderie

Karate is an inclusive sport welcoming people from all walks of life. The right kokoro fosters a spirit of inclusion, promoting unity and camaraderie among practitioners. You become an ambassador for the sport and help spread its values beyond the dojo.

The Right Kokoro Helps You Find Inner Peace

Karate is not merely about winning medals and competitions. It is about finding inner peace and balance. The right kokoro helps you do just that. When you have a clear mind, a pure heart, and a focused spirit, you connect with your inner being and achieve serenity, positively impacting other areas of your life.

The importance of having the right kokoro in karate cannot be overstated. It goes beyond physical training and enables you to become a well-rounded practitioner in mind and body. A clear and focused kokoro helps you overcome challenges, develop your technique, connect with your training partners, promote unity, and find inner peace. To take your karate practice to the next level, focus on cultivating the right Kokoro and watch your performance soar.

Psychological Aspects of Karate

Karate is more than a series of punches, kicks, and blocks—it's a way of life. Beyond the physical benefits of karate, like improved fitness and self-defense skills, martial arts can have profound psychological effects. This section explores the psychological aspects of karate and how practicing this ancient art benefits you mentally and physically.

Mental Fortitude

Firstly, karate cultivates discipline and self-control. The mental fortitude required to become proficient in this martial art involves dedication, hard work, and perseverance. The practice of karate is a pathway to understanding the power of the mind and how it can be harnessed to overcome obstacles. A sense of purpose and achievement comes with mastering a new technique or belt level carrying over into all aspects of life and giving practitioners control over their destinies.

Support System

Secondly, karate fosters a sense of community and belonging. Practicing karate alongside others pursuing the same goal creates a support system beyond the dojo. This sense of camaraderie and belonging leads to improved self-esteem and greater well-being. Additionally, karate offers an opportunity to connect with traditions and cultures practiced for centuries so practitioners feel more grounded and connected to a larger community.

Coping Mechanism

Thirdly, karate builds resilience and mental toughness. Even the most experienced karateka (karate experts) have setbacks in the dojo and life. The practice of karate helps individuals develop the coping mechanisms necessary to weather these challenges and come out stronger on the other side. This approach to adversity applies to any area of life and leads to more excellent emotional stability and a positive outlook on the world.

Stress Reduction

Fourthly, karate promotes mindfulness and stress reduction. The practice of karate requires complete presence at the moment, helping practitioners experience greater focus and concentration in all areas of life. Additionally, karate provides a healthy outlet for stress and anxiety, which is especially beneficial for individuals in high-stress professions or those dealing with mental health challenges. The physical release of energy helps individuals feel more relaxed and at ease.

Spiritual Growth

Finally, karate offers a path to personal and spiritual growth. Whether through meditation, breathing exercises, or kata (prearranged movements), karate provides opportunities for self-reflection and personal development. This approach helps individuals explore their values, beliefs, and goals, leading to greater self-awareness and a more profound sense of purpose.

The psychological aspects of karate provide an avenue for personal growth and development beyond the physical benefits of martial art. It offers a way to cultivate discipline, mental toughness, resilience, and mindfulness while fostering a sense of community and belonging so that individuals thrive inside and outside the dojo. So, whether your goal is to improve your physical fitness, learn self-defense, or explore what karate offers, the psychological benefits of this ancient art are undeniable.

The Four Mindsets

One of the crucial elements of karate is a mindset, the four perspectives: Shoshin, Mushin, Fudoshin, and Zanshin. Understanding these mindsets can improve your karate practice and your daily life. So, let's explore each perspective, its significance, and how to develop it.

Shoshin

Shoshin is the beginner's mind. It means having an open mind, free of preconceptions, opinions, or biases. When you approach karate or any learning experience with Shoshin, you become receptive to new ideas, willing to learn from your mistakes, and humble enough to ask for help. Shoshin is the foundation of continuous growth and improvement. You must let go of your ego, breathe deeply, and focus on the present moment to develop Shoshin. Practice karate as if practicing for the first time, with curiosity and enthusiasm rather than automatic habits.

Mushin

Mushin is the mind of no mind. It means being in a state of flow where your actions are spontaneous, intuitive, and effortless. Mushin refers to an empty mind, free of distractions, doubts, or fears, where you act instinctively and confidently. Mushin is the goal of all martial arts practice, where body and mind become one, and you react instantly and appropriately to any situation. To develop Mushin, you must be fully immersed in your practice and free from external or internal distractions. You must create your intuitive sense and trust your body's natural reactions.

Fudoshin

Fudoshin is the immovable mind. It means having a calm, stable, and committed mindset, regardless of external circumstances. Fudoshin refers to a warrior's spirit, where you are prepared for challenges and unshaken by obstacles or setbacks. Fudoshin is essential in karate when facing opponents trying to intimidate or distract you. You must simultaneously train your mind to be unyielding and flexible to develop Fudoshin. You must cultivate mental toughness, focus on breathing, and visualize yourself as invincible.

Zanshin

Zanshin is the lingering mind. It means having an aware, observant, and reflective mind, even after an action. Zanshin refers to a state of heightened awareness where you remain vigilant, watchful, and prepared for follow-up action. In karate, Zanshin is crucial, as it allows you to anticipate a counterattack, escape, or defense. Zanshin is also applicable in daily life to remain vigilant and attentive to your surroundings, even after completing a task. You must train your mind to be mindful, observant, and reflective to develop Zanshin. You must stay connected to your surroundings, focus on breathing, and visualize yourself as alert and ready.

The four mindsets in karate are more than abstract concepts or philosophical jargon. They are practical skills enhancing your karate practice and life. By developing Shoshin, you become receptive to new ideas and continuously improve. By creating Mushin, you are in a state of flow and instantly react to a situation. By developing Fudoshin, you become resilient and unyielding in the face of challenges. Finally, by creating Zanshin, you are always aware and vigilant. So, cultivate these mindsets, and see how your karate and your life transform.

Karate Styles and Techniques

Karate is a martial art that has evolved from ancient Japanese traditions. It involves punching, kicking, and striking techniques for defensive purposes. Karate has various styles and designs depending on the region and instructor. As a result, you might be overwhelmed by multiple styles and designs if you're new to karate. To help you get started, here are some of the main karate styles and techniques you should know:

- **Shotokan Karate:** Shotokan is one of the most popular styles of karate. It emphasizes powerful and straight movements, with punches and kicks delivered linearly. In addition, Shotokan focuses strongly on stances and breathing techniques, which develop strength and stamina.
- **Wado-Ryu Karate:** Wado-Ryu is another popular style of karate. It emphasizes quick movements and evasion techniques. Wado-Ryu focuses on body shifting and positioning, allowing the practitioner to maximize strength and speed.
- **Goju-Ryu Karate:** Goju-Ryu is a karate style focusing on circular movements and body conditioning. It emphasizes close-range combat techniques, including grappling and joint locks. Goju-Ryu strongly focuses on breathing techniques, improving cardiovascular health, and enhancing the body's natural healing abilities.
- **Kyokushin Karate:** Kyokushin is a karate style emphasizing full-contact sparring and physical conditioning. It strongly emphasizes powerful strikes and hardening the body through repeated impact training. Kyokushin incorporates throws, joint locks, and powerful kicks to the body and legs.
- **Bunkai:** Bunkai is not a karate style but a set of techniques to practice karate moves in a realistic, self-defense context. Bunkai involves breaking down the movements of Kata (a prearranged set of actions) and practicing them with a partner. It emphasizes practical self-defense techniques that can be used in real-world situations.

Karate is a diverse and exciting martial art with a range of styles and techniques to explore. However, regardless of which type you practice, the benefits of karate are numerous. From improving physical fitness to developing self-discipline and self-defense skills, karate has something to offer everyone.

Three Basic Elements of Karate

Karate is an ancient Japanese martial art popular worldwide. The word "karate" means "empty hand," meaning the martial art does not rely on weapons. Instead, karate relies on three essential elements: kihon, kata, and kumite. These elements are crucial for every beginner to learn and master. They form the foundation of karate and every other martial art. This section explains these three essential elements of karate in detail so you can improve your skills and become a better karateka.

Kihon

The first and most important essential element of karate is kihon. It means "basic techniques" and includes different blocks, punches, strikes, kicks, and stances. Kihon is the foundation of karate and helps develop proper body alignment, balance, and coordination. Therefore, a karateka must master kihon before moving on to more advanced techniques. A karateka can perform the other two elements effectively with overwhelming kihon.

Kata

The second essential element of karate is Kata. Kata means "form" and is a series of prearranged movements simulating a fight against imaginary opponents. Each kata has a specific sequence of activities, and every move has a purpose. Kata helps develop muscle memory, timing, rhythm, and breathing. Practicing kata improves a karateka's balance, coordination, and focus. Remember, kata should not be performed mechanically but with spirit, emotion, and expression.

Kumite

The third fundamental element of karate is Kumite. Kumite means "sparring" and is karate's most dynamic and exciting element. Kumite is a simulated fight with a partner and the ultimate test of a karateka's skills. Kumite develops reflexes, timing, speed, and agility. It teaches a karateka how to react in a real fight situation. However, kumite should not be taken lightly, as it can be dangerous if not performed correctly. Therefore, a karateka must always practice kumite safely and under the supervision of a qualified instructor.

How to Master These Elements

You must continuously practice and refine your skills to become a skilled karateka. An excellent way to practice kihon is to repeat each technique until it becomes automatic. Practice kata by memorizing the sequence of movements and performing them with emotion and expression. You can practice kumite by sparring with a partner and gradually increasing the intensity of the fight. A karateka must practice breathing techniques, meditation, and visualization to improve their focus, relaxation, and mental clarity.

Karate is a martial art requiring dedication, perseverance, and patience to master. By mastering the three essential elements of karate, a beginner can develop a strong foundation for their karate journey. These elements are interconnected, and by learning one aspect, a karateka improves the others. Remember, always practice safely and under the guidance of a qualified instructor. Keep practicing, and never give up on your karate journey.

This chapter explored the karate mindset and how it is essential in martial art. From the four mindsets of Shoshin, Mushin, Fudoshin, and Zanshin to the four main karate styles of Shotokan, Wado-Ryu, Kyokushin, and Goju-Ryu, you must have the right attitude and approach to become a better karateka. Furthermore, the three essential elements of Kihon, Kata, and Kumite were discussed in detail so karateka could practice and refine their skills. A karateka can become a skilled martial artist with dedication, perseverance, and patience.

Chapter 2: Kihon I Stances and Blocks

Karate is a martial art that has gained popularity across the globe thanks to its unique techniques and intense training regimen. One of the fundamental aspects of karate is mastering the kihon. These stances and blocks are the building blocks for all other karate techniques, making them essential to any practitioner's training. From the robust and rooted Zenkutsu Dachi stance to the elegant twists and turns of Hidari Gedan Barai, each kihon requires discipline, focus, and an unwavering commitment to excellence. Students can perfect these moves through extensive practice, increasing agility, coordination, and overall strength.

This chapter introduces you to the basic karate stances and blocks. It guides how to practice them properly and highlights their importance in proper training. When you master the core kihon, you open yourself to more advanced techniques. The confidence gained through only a few months of practice can last a lifetime. By the end of this chapter, you will be well-versed in basic karate stances and blocks. The aspect of karate will seem much less intimidating and more achievable.

Stances

Karate is not just about throwing punches and kicks. It's about mastering the art of stances. Known as Tachikata, stances are the foundation of every move and technique in karate. Each stance requires precise alignment and balance, from the classic front stance to the more advanced horse stance. It is essential to hold the stances correctly and move between them with speed and ease. When executed perfectly, stances give karate practitioners the power, speed, and flexibility to perform any move effectively.

Tachikata and Requirements

With its origins traced back to Japan, karate has become a widely practiced sport with millions of devotees worldwide. Known for its strength and lethal strikes, karate emphasizes the importance of a good stance in executing powerful punches and kicks. This section explores the basics of Tachikata and the requirements for a good stance in karate.

Basic Stances

Tachikata, or karate stance, forms the foundation of all the movements in karate. A good stance is essential in karate since it provides balance and stability to the body, which is critical in generating power for strikes. There are three basic stances in karate: Zenkutsu-dachi, Kiba-dachi, and Kokutsu-dachi. The Zenkutsu-dachi stance, known as the front stance, is the most common in karate. It involves placing one foot forward and the other back, with your knees bent and weight distributed evenly between the legs.

The Kiba-dachi, or horse stance, is standing with your feet shoulder-width apart and knees bent as if you were sitting on an imaginary chair. The Kokutsu-dachi stance, known as the back stance, requires you to stand with one foot back and the other foot forward, with your body leaning backward.

Achieving a Good Stance

Practitioners must meet specific requirements to achieve a good stance in karate. First, you must maintain proper balance by keeping your center of gravity low and distributing your weight between your legs. Your hips should be tucked in and aligned with your spine, and your back should be straight. Finally, controlling your breathing, inhaling deeply through the nose, and exhaling slowly through the mouth is imperative.

Secondly, foot placement is crucial to developing a good stance in karate. The distance between your feet and the angle of your toes must be adjusted for each stance. The foot placed at the front should be pointed toward the intended target, while the rear foot should be angled slightly to the side, providing stability and balance.

Thirdly, the knee position is vital in achieving a good stance. Your knees must be bent, but not too much that they extend past your toes, as this can put too much strain on the knee joints. Be mindful of your knee alignment with your toes; they should always point in the same direction.

Furthermore, your hands should be positioned at the right height in a good karate stance. The hands should be held up to protect the face, with the elbows tucked in to save the ribs. Avoid dropping your hands as it weakens the defense. Finally, maintaining eye contact and focus is crucial for a good karate stance. Your gaze should be permanently fixed on your opponent, allowing you to anticipate incoming strikes and react quickly.

Types of Stances

Karate techniques are rooted in a solid stance, providing stability to the practitioner, and channeling the power generated from the ground up. Stances are much more than just standing or walking in karate. They're the foundation of every move you execute. Therefore, understanding the various karate stances is crucial for any student aspiring to master the art. This section dives deep into the four stances in karate, their benefits, and how to execute them correctly.

Natural Stance

Heiko-Dachi, the natural stance.

The natural stance is karate's most important stance and the starting position for most moves. It's a simple yet effective stance characterized by your feet being shoulder-width apart, toes pointed straight ahead, and knees slightly bent. This is your default stance and the position you'll return to after each move. The natural stance sets the foundation for balance, strength, and mobility. Keep your core engaged and distribute your weight evenly on the balls of your feet. Remember to keep your head up, shoulders relaxed, and chin tucked in, facing straight ahead. This stance particularly benefits beginners, as it helps develop coordination and balance.

Unstable Stance

Kiba-dachi, the unstable stance

Unstable stances, known as kiba-dachi, require placing your feet further apart, with your toes pointing outward. This stance focuses on developing your leg strength, stability, and balance. This stance can lower your center of gravity, allowing you to generate more power for techniques like punches. Place your heels together; toes pointed out about 45 degrees, shift your weight back on your heels, and bend your knees evenly. Keep your back straight, chin tucked in, and your core engaged. This stance is particularly beneficial when delivering strikes with the feet or engaging in close-range combat.

Outside Tension Stance

Outside tension stance

The outside tension stance, or soto-tension, is more advanced. This stance is about maximizing the power of your techniques by creating tension in your muscles. Turn your front foot out to a 45-degree angle and push the heel of your back foot away from your body while keeping your toes on the ground. The movement engages your hips and core, emphasizing your side muscles. It stresses the lower back, hip joints, and leg muscles. The outside tension stance improves kicking ability, including high and spinning kicks. Additionally, it creates a more comprehensive, longer, and stable base that strengthens the lower body.

Inside Tension Stance

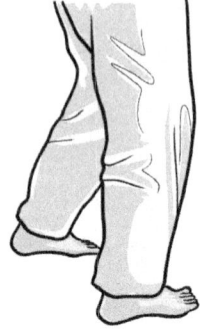 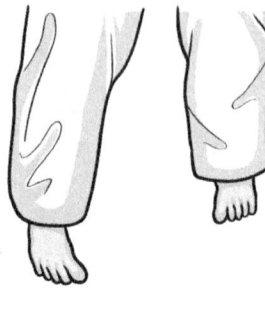

Uchi-tension stance

The inside tension stance, or uchi-tension, is like the outside tension stance but with the placement of the front foot reversed. It emphasizes the inner muscles, creating tension from your buttocks to the lower abs. It puts more pressure on your knees, making it a great stance for developing stability and power. The primary emphasis is mobility and to quickly move your hips and legs. Place your front foot at a 45-degree angle but position the back foot facing straight ahead. Lower yourself into the pose by bending your back foot knee. Ensure your back is straight and your head is up. This stance is ideal for offensive moves, like knee strikes and close-ranged techniques.

The natural and unstable stances are beginner-level stances that help develop coordination, flexibility, and balance. In addition, they allow the practitioner to generate power for strikes and kicks. On the other hand, the outside and inside tension stances are more advanced for offensive and defensive techniques. These stances emphasize the side and inner muscles, creating tension that channels energy to the hips, legs, and core. The correct execution of stances is crucial in karate, as it is the key to mastering powerful and decisive moves. With the proper technique and practice, perfecting the different stances in karate can take your game to the next level.

Stability in Karate

As a karate practitioner, mastering stability is a crucial aspect of the art, as it enables you to transfer your body weight effectively, control movements, and deliver precise blows. Unfortunately, karate practitioners often focus on techniques, forgetting that stability is the foundation of a successful attack or defense. This section explores practical tips and tricks to help you achieve stability in karate, from lowering your center of gravity to positioning your knees, ankles, soles, and hips.

Lowering the Center of Gravity

Lowering your center of gravity helps you stabilize your movements and maintain a balanced stance. This technique relies on bending your knees and dropping your hips slightly, allowing your body weight to spread evenly across both legs. To achieve this technique, do the following:

1. Start from a natural standing position and bend your knees, picturing yourself sitting on an imaginary chair.
2. Keep your feet hip-width apart, aligning them with your shoulder blades.
3. Engage your core muscles by pulling your belly button into your spine and exhaling slowly.
4. Distribute your weight evenly between both feet and avoid leaning too far forward or backward (keep your back straight).
5. Regularly practice this stance until it feels natural and comfortable. The lower your center of gravity, the more stable your movements will be.

Positioning Knees, Ankles, Soles, and Hips

Proper positioning of your knees, ankles, soles, and hips significantly contributes to stability in karate. Your knees should point in the same direction as your toes, and your ankles should remain flexible and relaxed. Your sole should grip the ground, allowing you to pivot and turn during techniques. Your hips should rotate smoothly, following the movements of your upper body. Stand sideways in front of a mirror and perform a basic punch to test your positioning. Watch your knees, ankles, soles, and hips, and correct any misalignment. Good habits in your stance will positively impact your overall stability and technique.

Do's and Don'ts

To further enhance your stability in karate, here are some do's and don'ts to consider:

- Keep your shoulders relaxed and your chin tucked in to avoid neck tension.
- Don't lock your joints or hyper-extend your limbs, which could cause instability and injury.
- Engage your core muscles and breathe deeply to increase stability and focus.
- Remember to warm up before training to prevent muscle strains and stiffness.
- Practice on different surfaces, such as soft ground or sand, to challenge your stability and balance.
- Take your time with your techniques and movements, ensuring stability and precision.

Mental Stability

Mental stability is as important as physical stability in karate. Mental strength is developing a clear, focused mind, free of distractions and negative thoughts. Practice meditation and mindfulness regularly, visualize your goals, and stay motivated to achieve mental stability. Use positive affirmations and celebrate small achievements along the way. Mental stability will improve your martial arts abilities and overall well-being.

Breathing Techniques for Karate

Karate is a martial art that involves a great deal of physical exertion, speed, and precision. You must master many techniques, including breathing, to become a skilled karate practitioner. Proper breathing techniques help generate power, focus the mind, and maintain balance. This section discusses breathing techniques for karate to improve your performance and take you one step closer to mastering this exciting martial art.

- **Abdominal Breathing**: Abdominal breathing, known as belly breathing, is an essential breathing technique in karate. It involves breathing through your nose, filling your belly with air, and exhaling through your mouth. This technique helps maintain a steady flow of oxygen to the muscles, increasing stamina and reducing fatigue. It calms the mind and regulates the heart rate.

- **Reverse Breathing:** Reverse breathing is a technique that involves inhaling while contracting the abdominal muscles and exhaling while expanding them. This technique helps generate extra power during strikes and blocks and strengthens the core muscles. However, this technique requires proper guidance as it can lead to dizziness and fainting if not performed correctly.

- **Breath Control:** Breath control is an essential aspect of karate. It involves synchronizing your breathing with your movements. For example, you could inhale while raising your arms and exhale while delivering a punch. This technique improves balance and coordination, making your movements more fluid and efficient.

- **Ki Breathing:** Ki breathing is meditation involving deep relaxation and controlled breathing. This technique increases your awareness of Ki, the life energy flowing through your body. Ki breathing involves inhaling slowly and deeply through the nose, holding the breath for a few seconds, and exhaling slowly through the mouth. This technique calms the mind, reduces stress, and improves overall health and well-being.

- **Dynamic Breathing:** Dynamic breathing uses short, sharp exhalations when striking or blocking. This technique increases power and speed and helps intimidate opponents. Dynamic breathing involves exhaling with force through the mouth while tightening the abdominal muscles. It is essential to practice this technique regularly to avoid hyperventilation.

Breathing techniques are an essential aspect of karate, and mastering them helps you improve your performance and achieve your goals. Whether a beginner or an experienced practitioner, incorporating these breathing techniques into your training routine helps you develop a deeper understanding of the art and takes your skills to the next level. Remember, practice these techniques slowly and steadily, and always seek guidance from a qualified instructor before attempting advanced techniques. With consistent practice and patience, you can become a karate master and take control of your mind, body, and spirit.

Blocks (Uke)

Karate is best known for its uke.
Martin Rulsch, Wikimedia Commons, CC BY-SA 4.0, CC BY-SA 4.0
<*https://creativecommons.org/licenses/by-sa/4.0*>, via Wikimedia Commons:
https://commons.wikimedia.org/wiki/File:K1PL_Berlin_2018-09-16_Female_Kata_108.jpg

Karate is an ancient martial art known for its powerful blocks (uke). The primary purpose of a block is to defend against an attacker's strikes and kicks. Karate blocks are not just simple movements but a combination of technique, speed, and power. This section delves deeper into the world of blocks, their types, and their importance in karate.

Basics

Blocks are among the fundamental techniques of karate, and every beginner must master them. A block, or "uke," is a defensive movement protecting the defender from attack. The most common blocks in karate are the rising block (age uke), inward block (uchi uke), outward block (soto uke), and downward block (gedan barai). Each block is crucial, and a karateka must master them all.

The rising block (age uke) is a rising motion deflecting an upward attack. The inward block (uchi uke) raises the forearm to block incoming punches or strikes. The outward block (or soto uke) deflects blows from the outside, and the downward block (gedan barai) aims to defend against low kicks and attacks.

Another essential block is the combination block, combining several individual blocks in rapid succession to defend against an attacker's continuous assaults. Combination blocking is crucial in modern-day karate, and a karateka must practice different combinations to react instinctively to an attacker's movements.

The importance of blocks in karate cannot be overstated. Besides protecting the defender from an attack, mastering blocks in karate provides the karateka with many benefits. Practicing blocks improves your muscle strength, speed, and flexibility, making it easier for you to execute more complex techniques. Blocks improve awareness and reaction time, essential qualities in martial arts.

A karateka must practice blocks regularly to perfect their techniques. Regular practice sessions should include warm-up exercises, drills, and sparring with an opponent to simulate a real-life attack. Practicing with a partner helps you to master defensive techniques while building confidence and learning to react instinctively.

Each block, ranging from inward and outward blocks to combination blocks, aims to protect the defender from an attacker's attack. Blocks provide countless benefits to the karateka, including improved muscle strength, speed, flexibility, awareness, and reaction time. Therefore, regular practice and training are essential for a karateka to master blocks and other karate techniques.

Timing the Blocks

Karate is a martial art focusing on self-defense techniques. Therefore, it requires much practice and discipline to master the various moves and techniques. This section discusses how to time your blocks and turn them into effective counterattacks in karate. This technique is crucial for martial artists because it can give you the upper hand in a fight and help you defend yourself effectively.

Timing Is Everything

Timing techniques will make or break your game. Timing blocks are essential to stopping the opponent from attacking you, but timing blocks and turning them into counterattacks is even better. When you time your blocks just right, you can land an effective counterpunch and subdue your opponent. You must stay focused and watch your opponent's movement and body language to time your blocks correctly. If you time your block too early or too late, your block could be ineffective, and your opponent will have an opportunity to attack you.

Striking Back

Once you timed your block correctly, it's time to strike back. When you counterattack, you take advantage of the momentum your opponent has generated and use it to your advantage. You should aim for vulnerable points like the ribs, throat, or groin to make your counterattack effective. These areas are sensitive and can cause immense pain to your opponent. When you land an effective counterattack, your opponent might be forced to back off, allowing you to escape or launch another attack.

Turning Blocks to Counterattacks

Timing blocks and turning them into counterattacks requires a lot of practice. The best way to practice is to pair up with a partner and practice different moves and techniques. During the practice session, your partner will play the role of the attacker, and you, the defender. When your partner attacks, you must focus on timing your block correctly and immediately launch a counterattack. You'll learn to time your blocks better with practice, and your counterattacks will become more effective.

Remember that timing blocks and turning them into counterattacks require patience and discipline. It would be best to wait for the right moment to strike and not rush into an attack. It takes a lot of practice to master the technique, so don't get discouraged if it doesn't work the first time. Keep practicing, and you'll eventually get better at it.

In addition to the basic blocks discussed in this chapter, a karateka can practice plenty of more advanced techniques. Blocks such as split blocks, cross blocks, and palm-heel blocks can further protect the defender from an attacker's attack. These techniques require more practice and skill but provide even more excellent protection once mastered. When practicing these advanced blocks, it is essential to keep the same principles of timing in mind. Correctly timing these blocks will ensure the defender's counterattack is more likely to succeed.

Maintaining a good stance is critical to effectively performing kicks, punches, and blocks. A proper stance requires Tanden or the center of gravity to be at the body's center. This ensures the weight is evenly distributed and the movements are precise. Good Tachikata differentiates a novice from a seasoned karateka, and regular practice can help improve their stance. Developing a balanced and stable posture is critical to advance in karate and is a journey worth undertaking. So, kick off your shoes, stand up tall, and let's get ready to strike the perfect stance.

Chapter 3: Kihon II Punches and Kicks

Punches and kicks are just a tiny part of what makes karate so forward-thinking. When you watch a skilled karate practitioner, you'll observe that their movements are almost effortless yet incredibly powerful. Likewise, the kicks and punches in karate are meant to be quick and deadly, making karate highly effective in self-defense. Mastering the karate techniques takes time, but understanding the basics is an essential starting point.

This chapter breaks down the basics of karate punches and kicks so that you can confidently begin your karate journey. First, it covers the essential grips and punches, from simple straight punches and jabs to advanced techniques like reverse punches and katas. Second, you learn the basics of kicking, from front kicks to crescent and reverse crescent kicks. Finally, it touches on advanced karate kicks, leg attacks, and non-traditional kicks.

Punches

From the classic front punch to the roundhouse and uppercut, karate is a martial art where the power of the punch reigns supreme. Each punch requires precision and technique to execute flawlessly, making it all the more satisfying when you finally master them. You won't forget the adrenaline rush from throwing a punch in sparring or in a real fight. Karate punches seem intimidating, but they can become one of your greatest weapons with practice and dedication. So, put on those gloves, channel your inner karate master, and get started.

Holding a Punch Grip

Holding a punch is necessary for practicing karate.

Karate is a martial art involving striking, kicking, and punching techniques. The grip you use when punching is essential to the effectiveness of your striking techniques. It's necessary to have a solid punch grip in karate, as it contributes to the accuracy and power of your punches. This section explores the importance of holding a punch grip in karate, why it matters, and how to improve your punch grip technique.

Importance of a Punch Grip

A firm punch grip is essential in karate as it helps you build more power in your punching technique. The more muscle you put into your punches, the more you intimidate your opponents and offer a quick victory. A punch grip can also be an indicator of your technique. A correct punch grip will demonstrate your mastery of the method.

Improving Your Punch Grip

One way to improve your punch grip in karate is by strengthening the muscles in your hand. Hand-gripping devices can help, or even simple exercises like squeezing a tennis ball or gripping resistance bands. You can improve your grip by focusing on the position of your fingers. For example, they should be positioned close together in a fist. It ensures you make contact with your knuckles on the punching bag and protect them from injury.

Tips for Holding a Punch Grip

During karate practice, it's crucial to maintain a loose punch grip to prevent injury. With a loose grip, your hand can quickly adapt to the movement of the punch and prevent your wrist from injury. In addition, you must ensure your wrist is straight during the punch, as bending your wrist can damage the tendons. Furthermore, the angle of your wrist and the flexibility in your hand should remain consistent throughout each punch. Lastly, tuck your thumb away firmly at all times. Keeping your thumb out of the way prevents it from getting injured as you punch.

Perfect Punch Grip

A perfect punch grip in karate is natural and comfortable. Your grip should provide enough power to break boards. However, avoid gripping tightly, which will result in damaged knuckles and injury. Instead, aim to strike at the correct angle, with your knuckles aimed at the target. With the proper technique, it will become second nature. Focus on strengthening the muscles in your hands, positioning your fingers correctly, and maintaining a loose grip to improve your punch grip. During karate practice, master the art of the punch with a firm punch grip and good technique; your punches will have greater power, accuracy, and a good chance of success.

Four Basic Punches

Karate emphasizes punches as one of its primary striking techniques. The art of karate is known for its powerful and precise punches that can bring an opponent to the ground in one strike. This section discusses the four basic punches in karate to unleash your full potential as a practitioner. Mastering these punches will improve your physical strength and cultivate mental discipline.

Straight Punch

The Seiken punch is fundamental in karate.

The straight punch, known as the "Seiken" punch, is the most fundamental in karate. It involves striking with a straightened arm and pushing forward with your body weight. This punch is aimed at your opponent's face, solar plexus, or ribs. When performing a straight punch, keep your elbows close to your torso and turn your wrist at the end of the punch to add more force. Mastering this technique requires a lot of practice, focusing on perfecting your posture, balance, and timing.

Lunge Punch

Oi-Zuki is more powerful than a straight punch.

The lunge punch, known as the "Oi-Zuki" punch, is more potent than the straight punch. It involves stepping forward with one foot while throwing a punch simultaneously. The force generated in this technique comes from your body's momentum as you lunge forward. Aim for your opponent's chest or stomach with this punch. Keep your back straight and rotate your back foot as you punch to achieve maximum power. This technique is more advanced than the straight punch and requires more training in speed and accuracy.

Reverse Punch

Gyaku-Zuki generates more power and speed than a straight punch.

The reverse punch, known as the "Gyaku-Zuki," is thrown from the hip. This punch can cause more damage than the straight punch since it generates more power and speed. To execute this technique, turn your back foot 90 degrees and twist your hip, creating torque in your body. The punch is delivered in a straight line, aimed at your opponent's ribcage or head. The reverse punch is a signature move in karate and can knock down your opponent in one blow with correct execution.

Jab Punch

Oi-Tsuki can be used as a setup for other punches.

The jab punch, known as the "Oi-Tsuki," is a quick, sharp punch to distract your opponent. It is often thrown as a setup to other punches or as a counterpunch to the opponent's jab. This technique is executed by extending your arm straight and quickly retracting it, aiming for the opponent's face. Keep your elbow close to your torso and snap your fist back to its starting position. This punch is a valuable tool for sparring since it can disorient the opponent and provide openings for other attacks.

Karate is an art requiring years of training and discipline, but mastering the four basic punches is the foundation of becoming a skilled karateka. The straight punch, lunge punch, reverse punch, and jab punch are techniques every student must learn to become proficient in karate. These techniques help build strength, speed, and precision and are used during sparring or self-defense. Remember, practice these techniques until they become intuitive, and you'll be well on your way to becoming a skilled karate practitioner.

Advanced Punches and Katas

Karate is more than just a discipline. It's developing your mindset, body, and spirit. As you progress in your training, you'll learn more powerful techniques and moves demanding precision, strength, and balance. This section explores advanced punches and katas in karate. Whether you're a veteran or a newbie, you'll find valuable insights to help unleash your power and elevate your skills.

Mechanics of Advanced Punches

Punching is one of the basic karate skills, but it takes years of practice and dedication to master. In advanced karate, punches become more complex and powerful. The key is to use your entire body, not just your fist, to generate maximum force and speed. You must coordinate your breath, stance, and hips to deliver a punch to knock down your opponent. Some of the advanced punches in karate include the reverse punch, double punch, and spinning back fist. You must train your muscles, reflexes, and timing to execute these punches. Work with your sensei or instructor to learn the proper technique and gradually increase intensity and accuracy.

Kata: The Art of Moving Meditation

Kata is a sequence of movements simulating a fight against multiple opponents. It's a fundamental aspect of karate training, developing your coordination, balance, focus, and martial art skills. Kata requires precision, grace, and intensity. It's not just about moving your arms and legs randomly. Each movement has a purpose and meaning. It's like a dance telling a story. In advanced karate, kata becomes more complex and demanding. You must memorize longer and more intricate sequences and perform them with incredible speed and power. Kata is a physical, mental, and emotional exercise. It teaches you discipline, patience, and resilience.

Double-Hand, Fore-Knuckle, and Spear-Hand Punches

Now that you know the basics of punching, let's explore more advanced punches. These punches are crucial in fighting and self-defense situations. Learning them teaches you to throw a punch and deliver maximum impact properly. Here's a brief overview of each punch:

Double-Hand Punch

The double-hand punch is a technique used by many martial artists worldwide. It uses both hands to strike an opponent. To deliver this punch, you must execute a step forward with your lead foot bringing both hands to your chest. Then, thrust both hands forward while holding your fists together and planting your body weight behind your punch. This technique can cause significant damage to your opponent's organs, ribs, and spine. When executed correctly, this punch can deliver a knockout blow.

Fore-Knuckle Punch

The fore-knuckle punch is one of the most effective punches in martial arts. It is a technique involving striking an opponent with the knuckles of the index and middle fingers. To execute this punch, form a fist with your thumb on the outside of your fingers. Extend the knuckles of the index and middle fingers so that the fingers protrude forward to form a punch. Deliver this punch by thrusting your arm forward and leading with your shoulder. This punch can cause significant damage to your opponent's face, nose, and jawline. Therefore, accuracy and proper alignment are critical to maximizing this punch's impact.

Spear-Hand Punch

The spear-hand punch is a technique in which the hand is fashioned into a spear. It involves driving the fingertips straight into vulnerable regions of the opponent's torso. When executed with force, this punch can cause damage to vital organs, such as the solar plexus, liver, and heart. To perform the spear-hand punch, form a fist and extend your fingers forward, keeping your fingers straight and the thumb tucked alongside your index finger. Next, thrust your arm forward, pushing your fingertips toward your target while maintaining a rigid wrist.

The advantages of the spear-hand punch are that it is lightning-fast and more directly powerful than an ordinary hand strike. The key is to deliver this punch with a solid and stable forward drive to drive your fingers into your opponent's body. In addition, proper training of the wrist and forearm muscles to deliver an effective spear-hand punch is vital.

These three punches are very effective and must be learned by those wanting to be proficient in martial arts. They are versatile and can be used in various fighting and self-defense applications. However, these techniques should only be used in self-defense and never violently or aggressively. Hone your skills through constant practice and learning to execute these punches' powerfully. Master these techniques and become a more powerful martial artist willing to defend yourself and others.

Combining Punches and Katas

Punches and katas are like two sides of the karate coin. They complement each other and enhance your martial art skills. Combining punches and katas creates a dynamic and versatile training routine challenging your body and mind. You can incorporate different advanced punches into your kata sequences to add variety, strength, and surprise. You can use katas as a warm-up or a cool-down before or after a punch session. The key is to balance punches and katas and avoid overusing or underusing each element.

Training Tips for Advanced Punches and Katas

To improve your performance and avoid injuries, here are some tips for training to perform advanced punches and katas:

- Warm up properly before starting your training. Do some stretching, cardio, and joint mobility exercises.
- Focus on quality, not quantity. Don't rush your punches or katas. Instead, focus on the details and form.
- Progress gradually. Don't try to master all the advanced punches and katas at once. Instead, start with the basics and work your way up.

- Take breaks and rest between sessions. Your body needs time to recover and adapt to the stress of training.
- Listen to your body and your sensei. Don't push too hard or ignore your pain or discomfort. Instead, talk to your sensei about concerns or questions.

Kicks

Watching a skilled karate practitioner execute the perfect kick with graceful movements, precision, and lightning-fast speed is genuinely mesmerizing. It's like watching a work of art in motion. Moreover, karate kicks are incredibly effective self-defense tools. So, whether a beginner or a black belt, perfecting your kicks is essential to mastering the art of karate, but don't forget the fun factor. There's something incredibly satisfying about feeling the impact of your foot connecting with a target. It's a rush that keeps karate enthusiasts coming back for more. So, get your leg muscles fired up and your focus sharpened because this section dives deeper into karate kicks.

Key Tips for Kicking

- **Choose The Right Karate School:** The first and most crucial step in becoming a successful karateka is choosing the right karate school. There are many karate styles, so it is vital to find a school that teaches a style you are interested in. Additionally, finding a school with experienced and qualified instructors is essential.
- **Set Realistic Goals:** One of the biggest mistakes people make when starting karate is setting unrealistic goals. Remember, karate is a lifelong journey rather than something to master overnight. So, instead of setting goals like "I want to be a black belt in six months," set goals like "I want to attend class three times per week" or "I want to learn one new technique per week."
- **Be Patient:** karate takes time and patience to master. There will be days when you feel you are making significant progress and days when you feel you are not making any progress. It is essential to stick with it and be patient with yourself. Remember, every great skill needs nurturing at first.
- **Practice, Practice, Practice:** The only way to improve at karate is to practice regularly. In addition to attending class, it is essential

to practice at home. You can do this by shadowboxing, practicing techniques on a heavy bag, or even doing push-ups and sit-ups. The more you practice, the better you will become.

- **Stay Healthy And Injury-Free**: It is crucial to stay healthy and injury-free to be a master in karate. It means eating a balanced diet, sleeping well, and stretching before and after each training session. It is essential to listen to your body and rest when sore or tired.
- **Have Fun:** Remember, karate is supposed to be fun. If you are not enjoying yourself, then there is no point in doing it. Instead, find an activity you will enjoy, and have fun with it.

Essential Kicks to Master

Karate is a martial art known for its fast-paced movements, powerful strikes, and dynamic kicks. While there are many techniques in karate, mastering the different kicks is essential for any practitioner. However, with so many kicks to learn, it can take time to know where to start. This section reviews the essential kicks to master karate. Whether a beginner or seasoned martial artist looking to revisit the fundamentals, this guide will help you develop your skills and improve your performance.

- **Front Kick**: The front kick is one of the most basic kicks in karate, and often the first beginners learn. To perform a front kick, stand in a fighting stance with your dominant foot behind you. Lift your knee toward your chest and extend your leg, striking your opponent with the ball of your foot. Again, keeping your toes pointed up and your heel down is crucial to avoid injury.
- **Side Kick**: The side kick is powerful and can knock down your opponent if executed correctly. To perform a sidekick, lift your knee toward your chest and turn your body to face your target. Extend your leg out while keeping your toes pointed up and your heel down. Aim to kick with the blade of your foot, the area on the outer side of your foot.
- **Roundhouse Kick:** The roundhouse kick is a versatile kick targeting your opponent's head, torso, or legs. To perform a roundhouse kick, start in a fighting stance and lift your knee toward your chest. Then, pivot on your standing foot and kick out with your leg, aiming to hit your target with your shin. Retracting your leg quickly after striking is vital to avoid leaving

yourself open to counterattacks.

- **Crescent and Reverse Crescent Kicks:** Crescent and reverse crescent kicks are advanced techniques requiring a lot of practice to master. To perform a crescent kick, lift your knee toward your chest and extend your leg out while making a circular motion with your foot. The aim is to hit your opponent with the blade of your foot while swinging your leg around their head. Reverse crescent kicks are done in the opposite direction, with the leg hanging toward the back of your opponent's head.

Mastering different karate kicks takes time, practice, and dedication. So, whether you're learning basic front kicks or advanced crescent kicks, focus on the details, such as posture, foot position, and timing. By incorporating these essential kicks into your training routine, you'll become a well-rounded karate student and improve your technique and performance in the dojo. As always, remember to train safely and under the guidance of a qualified instructor.

Advanced Kicks and Leg Attacks

You must work hard on your kick's speed, power, and accuracy to be an excellent karate fighter. Training in advanced kicks and leg attacks in karate is a challenging but rewarding experience teaching you various techniques to keep your opponent guessing. This section explores the world of non-traditional kicks and leg attacks.

- **Spinning Back Heel Kick:** The standard kicks in karate, such as the front, roundhouse, and side kick, are well-known and commonly used, but there are plenty more kicks to add to your arsenal. The first non-traditional kick is the spinning back heel kick. Start by spinning and raising your back leg, then snap it around to kick your opponent with the heel of the foot. This kick is excellent as a surprise attack and for changing direction quickly.
- **Hook Kick:** Another effective kick is the hook kick or "Ura Mae Geri." Swing it in a circle using your back leg to generate momentum and extend your leg mid-swing into a kick. This kick is hard to see coming and for your opponent to block due to its unique motion. Please take advantage of this kick's unpredictability by using it at the right moment to confuse your opponent.

- **Low-Spinning Back Kick:** A low-spinning back kick is highly effective and underused. This kick sweeps low and can take down opponents by aiming at their ankles. To perform this kick, start in a low stance, spin to turn your back toward your opponent, and sweep their legs away from them with your heel.
- **Knee Kick:** Despite its name, the knee kick, or "Hiza Geri," is an incredibly effective attack when done correctly. The motion of the knee kick is excellent for delivering a devastating blow to your opponent's stomach or chest. To start the kick, bring your knee up toward your opponent's chest and extend your leg. It is essential to practice this non-traditional kick carefully; otherwise, you could injure your knee.
- **Stomp Kick:** Another overlooked kick that catches many fighters off guard is the "Fumikomi" or stomp kick. This kick is done by stepping with the lead leg and driving it down onto your opponent. A well-executed stomp kick can disrupt an opponent's movements or break their bones.

It would help if you had a wide-ranging collection of kicks and leg techniques to become an excellent karate fighter. The classic kicks are essential, but the non-traditional kicks discussed can catch your opponent off guard, confuse them, or lead them into a trap for your next move. Train thoroughly to make your moves as fast and accurately as possible and become a skilled karate fighter. You can master these advanced kicks and leg attacks and become a deadly karate fighter with lots of practice and dedication.

Readers can find a comprehensive glossary at the end of this guide covering all the topics discussed here. This glossary provides detailed information about each punch, kick, and attack discussed in this chapter. Now that you understand the basics of punches and kicks, the next chapter discusses white and yellow belt katas kumite.

Chapter 4: White and Yellow Belt Katas and Kumite

Karate belts are a fascinating component of the martial arts tradition that has captivated people for generations. The first two belts of the belt system, white and yellow, signify new beginnings, but they mark an important milestone in karate practice. Not only do they represent the first steps in a student's journey toward mastery, but they also come with unique challenges and rewards. Whether you're a beginner looking to take your first steps in karate or simply curious about the intricacies of a martial arts practice, the white and yellow belts are vivid reminders of the dedication and determination that go into mastering this fascinating craft.

This chapter focuses on the kata and kumite required for white and yellow belt karate practitioners. It explores the Heian Shodan, Heian Nidan, and Heian Sandan katas. It provides embusen/floor diagrams to help illustrate the flow of movements. The second part of this chapter looks at the Gohon Kumite and Sanbon Kumite. This chapter aims to give budding martial arts practitioners a clear understanding of the basics to build solid foundations and progress in their training.

Katas

As a beginner in the karate world, white and yellow belt katas seem daunting at first but don't worry. These katas teach the fundamental moves and techniques of karate while also honing your focus and concentration. Whether practicing the basic punches and kicks or moving into more complex sequences, correctly executing the katas improves your physical abilities and provides an incredible mental workout. As you progress through your training, you'll look back on your early belt katas with pride and appreciation for the solid foundation they provided. Here are the three katas you'll be focusing on:

Heian Shodan

Heian Shodan

Performing the Heian Shodan.

Karate is not just a physical art form; it is also an expression of mental and spiritual prowess practiced and refined over centuries. Kata, a legendary practice of karate, is a unique collection of martial art movements honing a karateka's strength, endurance, and flexibility. Heian Shodan Kata is the first Kata of the Heian Kata series and among the most popular katas in karate, particularly among beginners. This section explores the intricacies of Heian Shodan Kata, how to execute it flawlessly, and its significance in karate.

Heian Shodan Kata comprises 21 movements that must be executed in a specific sequence. Each movement must be completed with precision and focus. The kata begins with the "Ready" posture, followed by the "Kamae" posture and "Oi Tsuki" movements. The "Oi Tsuki" movement is a forward punch aimed at an imaginary opponent.

The "Gedan Barai" movement comes next, a sweeping downward motion, followed by the "Age Uke" movement. The "Age Uke" motion is an upward block aimed toward the face of the imaginary opponent. Next, the "Gedan Barai" movement is repeated in the opposite direction, followed by the "Shuto Uke" movement and "Oi Tsuki" again. The "Shuto Uke" movement is a Knife-hand block aimed toward the neck area of the opponent.

In the Heian Shodan kata, are several leg movements, such as the "Kekomi" and "Mawashi Geri" kicks, requiring perfect execution, as a fault could lead to a disastrous outcome. Moreover, every movement must be completed precisely and with perfect timing, including the "Tate Zuki" movement involving a vertical punch aimed at the opponent's solar plexus.

Regularly practicing Heian Shodan Kata improves physical technique and provides a deeper understanding of the practical application of karate. The kata comprises different techniques like blocks, kicks, and punches, and every move must be executed with precision and focus. Perfecting the sequence of movements of this kata and correctly performing them leads to mastery. Explore the intricacies of this kata and embrace the beauty and discipline of karate.

Heian Nidan

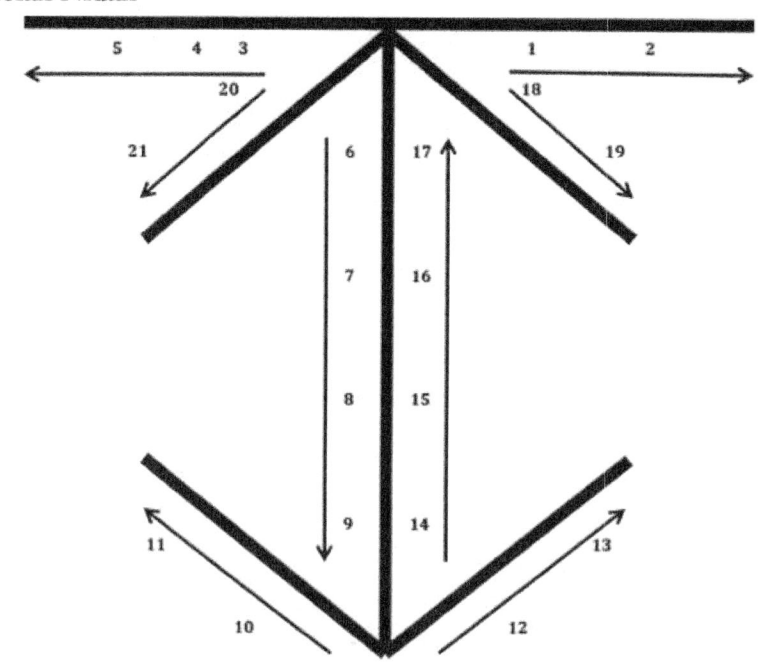

Heian Nidan movement pattern.
Haresh karate, CC BY-SA 4.0 <https://creativecommons.org/licenses/by-sa/4.0>, via Wikimedia Commons: https://commons.wikimedia.org/wiki/File:Karate_Kata_Heian_Nidan.jpg

Karate is self-defense and a way of life. Kata, like Heian Nidan, is an essential part of karate and helps students develop their self-defense skills, flexibility, and concentration. Although Heian Nidan is considered a fundamental kata in karate, it still requires practice, patience, and discipline to master. Anyone wanting to learn karate should start with Heian Nidan and focus on the basic movements before moving to other advanced katas. This section explores Heian Nidan Kata and explains how to perform it.

Heian Nidan Kata is the second kata in the Heian series, consisting of 26 movements. Heian means "peaceful mind," and Nidan represents "second level." The kata is relatively simple and is an excellent starting point for anyone learning karate. Here are the steps to perform Heian Nidan:

- **Step 1:** Starting Position. Stand still, bow to the front, and take a left footstep into Heisoku Dachi or a closed stance.
- **Step 2.** Chamber your right fist at your right hip and punch with your left hand on the left side. Move two steps forward while

punching.

- **Step 3:** Chamber your left hand by your left hip and punch with your right hand on the right side.
- **Step 4:** Bring your left foot into the Kiba Dachi stance and perform two consecutive lower-grade blocks, left then right, with the opposite-hand leg forward.
- **Step 5:** Rotate your left foot 90 degrees and step forward with your right into a forward stance with a simultaneous downward block with your right hand.
- **Step 6:** Without pausing, rotate your right foot 180 degrees to face backward, executing a right downward block.
- **Step 7:** Bring your left foot back, pivot your left foot to face backward, and move your right foot backward, transitioning to a new forward stance. Perform an overhead block with your left hand. Simultaneously, your right open hand will be pulled back behind to the right side of the hip.
- **Step 8:** Bring your feet together and move into the starting position, facing front.

The above steps are the first half of the kata. As mentioned earlier, Heian Nidan consists of 26 movements; every action is essential. It takes practice, focus, and discipline to understand and master the kata completely. Here are some additional steps you will perform when completing the kata:

- **Turn and Blocks:** From your starting stance, perform a series of turns and blocks to defend yourself against the imaginary assailants.
- **Kicks:** Perform various kicks, like Mae Geri, Kekomi, and Mawashi Geri. Proper balance and leg strength are essential for performing kicks.
- **Punches:** Like other katas in karate, Heian Nidan includes various punches, such as Age Uke, Yoko Uchi, and Uchi Uke.
- **Combination of Techniques:** You must display various techniques, including blocks, kicks, and punches. It requires focus and precision to perform all the movements correctly.

Heian Sandan

Heian Sandan

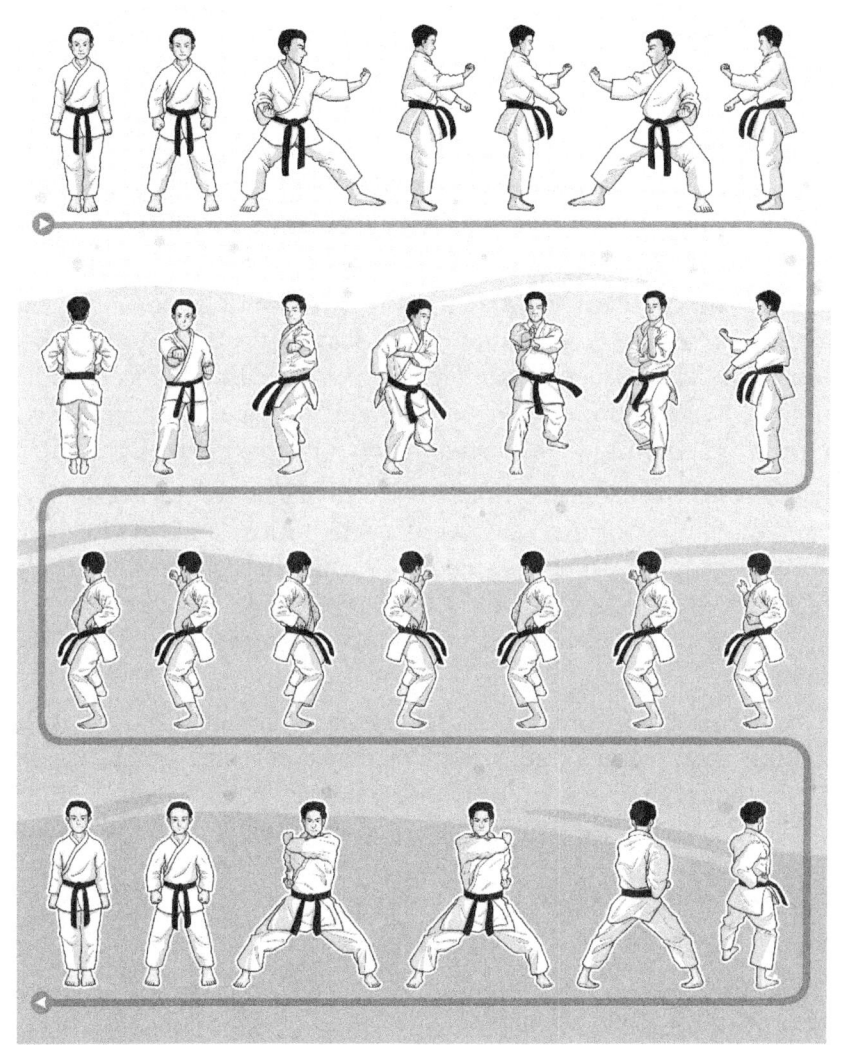

Heian Sandan is often considered a bridge between basic and advanced katas.

For karate practitioners, the Heian Sandan kata is an essential part of their training. This section explores the Heian Sandan kata, one of the five Heian Katas in karate. This kata is often called the "bridge" between the basic and more advanced katas. You will learn to perform this kata, its meaning, how to practice it, and its benefits in martial arts and everyday life.

The Heian Sandan kata consists of 20 movements to teach you powerful techniques, such as age uke (upper block), shuto uchi (knife-hand strike), and gedan barai (lower block). The kata starts with a step forward and a downward block, followed by a double punch. The arms are then raised, and you perform a knife-hand block and a reverse punch. Next, you perform a low block and a rising elbow strike.

As you continue through the kata, you perform various techniques, such as front kicks, strikes, and blocks. The Heian Sandan kata shows how to transition fluidly from one method to another and how to use the power generated from the hips to deliver effective strikes. This kata emphasizes timing, speed, and agility, essential elements in karate.

The Heian Sandan kata has a more profound significance beyond learning self-defense techniques. The kata reflects the spiritual and philosophical aspects of karate. It teaches humility, respect, and self-discipline. Every move should be executed with intention and focus as you strive to become a better karate practitioner and person overall.

It is vital to maintain good posture and balance to practice this, Kata. Focus on the transition between each move and perform each movement with precision and intent. Practice the kata slowly, gradually increasing your speed and power. It is helpful to practice the kata in front of a mirror to ensure your techniques are correct and monitor your progress.

The benefits of practicing the Heian Sandan kata go beyond becoming more robust and agile. Practicing this kata builds character, fosters self-discipline and respect, and enhances mental clarity and focus. The kata increases stamina and flexibility and improves overall physical fitness.

Kumites

Karate's appeal lies in its physical and mental challenges. Therefore, *kumite* (or sparring) is crucial to karate training. As a karate student, you have the opportunity to engage in kumites at various levels, beginning with the white belt learning and practicing basic techniques. Once you master the basic skills and graduate to the yellow belt, you will participate in more competitive kumites. This section discusses the white and yellow belt kumites, their rules, and how to train for them.

The white belt kumite is the starting level for the karateka. In the white belt kumite, you spar with a partner following predetermined techniques you learned in class. The kumite allows you to apply your learned techniques in a controlled and safe environment. The kumite helps you develop a strong fighting spirit and learn to fight respectfully and with good sportsmanship. The yellow belt kumite is the second level in the kumite progression. At this level, you engage in more competitive kumites. In the yellow belt, you fight against someone in the same belt level or higher. Yellow belt kumite focuses on developing good timing, rhythm, and distance. You learn to assess your opponent's movement and intents. The yellow belt kumite is an opportunity to take on a more challenging fight and learn to adapt to different fighting styles.

To practice for the kumites, you must improve stances, balance, and posture. Additionally, you must master basic techniques such as blocks, punches, and kicks. Practicing sparring with a partner, using protective gear like a karate gi and helmet, will help you simulate the kumite and test your skills. It would be best to practice hitting a makiwara, a punching bag, to develop strength in your punches and kicks.

The karate kumite provides a practical way to develop martial arts skills. The white and yellow belt kumites are great starting points for young karate enthusiasts. Along with learning basic techniques, students will understand the importance of sportsmanship. As you continue your journey in karate, you learn to adapt to different fighting styles and improve your fighting spirit. By practicing regularly and giving your best effort, you will progress to higher belt levels while enjoying the thrill of kumites.

Gohon Kumite

Gohon Kumite technique.

Karate is known for its rigorous training and demanding techniques, such as the Gohon Kumite. Gohon Kumite is a five-step sparring exercise for advancing karate students. It involves defending against five different attacks while responding with predetermined techniques.

You will need a partner to perform Gohon Kumite. The exercise should be performed at a steady pace, and it's essential to maintain control throughout. Here are the steps to achieving Gohon Kumite:

- **Step 1:** The first attack is a straight front punch. Your partner punches with their lead hand, and you block with your front arm, simultaneously stepping in with the opposite foot. Then counterattack with your lead punch.
- **Step 2:** The second attack is a lead roundhouse kick. Your partner throws a roundhouse kick at your ribs, and you block with your forearm, then step in and counterattack with a punch.
- **Step 3:** The third attack is a straight punch followed by a reverse punch combination. Your partner throws a straight punch with one hand, immediately following with a reverse punch with the opposite hand. You block the first punch with the opposite hand, the second with the same hand, step in, and counterattack with a punch.
- **Step 4:** The fourth attack is a lead front kick. Your partner throws a front kick at your chest. You block with your front arm while simultaneously stepping in with the opposite foot. Then counterattack with a punch.
- **Step 5:** The fifth and final attack is a simple grab and punch. Your partner grabs your front wrist and punches you with the opposite hand. You escape the wrist grab, block the punch with your opposite hand, and counterattack with a punch.

Gohon Kumite is an excellent technique for advancing karate students. It helps them gain control, improve their timing, and enhance their response to different attacks. Remember, approach the exercise steadily, maintain control, and focus on technique. With practice, you'll master Gohon Kumite in no time.

Sanbon Kumite

Karate uses strikes, kicks, and punches as self-defense mechanisms. Sanbon Kumite is commonly practiced in most schools. It is a three-step sparring technique to improve students' reflexes, agility, and coordination in real-world situations. This kumite requires basic techniques such as jabs, front kicks, and reverse roundhouse kicks. This section discusses the steps to perform Sanbon Kumite.

- **Step 1:** Starting Position: The starting position requires standing 6 feet from your opponent. The attacker and defender stand in a Sanchin Dachi stance with their hands up to their face. The attacker initiates the sparring by throwing a jodan punch toward the defender's face. The defender blocks the punch with a rising block and moves in for a punch of their own.

- **Step 2:** The First Exchange: After the initial block, the defender throws a jodan punch toward the attacker's face. The attacker blocks the punch with a rising block and returns with a chudan punch toward the defender's chest. The defender blocks the punch with a lower block, completing the exchange.

- **Step 3:** The Second Exchange: Once the first exchange is completed, the attacker initiates the second exchange with a gyaku-tsuki or reverse punch to the defender's solar plexus. The defender blocks the attack with an inside or outside block and counter-attacks with a Mae Geri or front kick. As the defender throws the front kick, they must keep the attacker at a distance and return to the starting position.

- **Step 4:** The Third Exchange: In the third exchange, the attacker initiates the sparring with a mawashi geri or roundhouse kick. The defender blocks the kick with a rising block and counterattacks with a gyaku-tsuki or reverse punch toward the attacker's face. The attacker blocks the punch with an inside or outside block and returns to the starting position.

- **Step 5:** Repeat the Process: Once the third exchange is over, the roles of the attacker and defender switch, and the steps are repeated. The defender becomes the attacker, and so on. This process is repeated thrice to help students master the Sanbon Kumite technique.

Sanbon Kumite is an essential technique in karate, improving a student's defensive and offensive sparring capabilities. By understanding and mastering the steps in this kumite, students establish fluidity in fighting and ultimately become better karatekas. It takes time and practice to perfect the Sanbon Kumite technique, but by following these steps, anyone can learn and execute it expertly. So, the next time you're in karate class, try out Sanbon Kumite and become a better martial artist.

As you begin your journey into the martial arts world, the white and yellow belt katas and kumite (sparring) are the foundation for your practice. These initial levels enable you to develop precise movements and defend yourself in real-life situations. Kata is a prearranged exercise allowing you to hone in on your technique and fluidity. As you move on to kumite, you'll face an opponent and focus on timing, distance, and strategy. Don't let the color of your belt discourage you. These basic skills are essential to advancing in martial arts and giving you the confidence to conquer any challenge. So, get ready to kick, punch, and chop your way to success.

Chapter 5: Orange and Green Belt Katas and Kumite

As karateka progresses through the ranks, they are introduced to a series of katas and kumite, which help them improve their technique and master the art of self-defense. Orange and green belt students are required to learn a specific set of katas and kumite to test their physical and mental abilities. These katas and kumite help the students become more disciplined, focused, and confident in their approach to karate. With rigorous training and consistent practice, students can progress to become black belts, the highest rank in karate.

If you're an aspiring karateka, ready to put in the effort and dedication to unleash your true potential, this chapter is for you. From the Heian Yondan to Kihon-Ippon Kumite, this chapter provides an in-depth look at the techniques orange and green belts learn to progress. In addition, it aims to give you a better understanding of the katas and kumite to master when training for the middle-order belt ranks.

Heian Yondan Kata

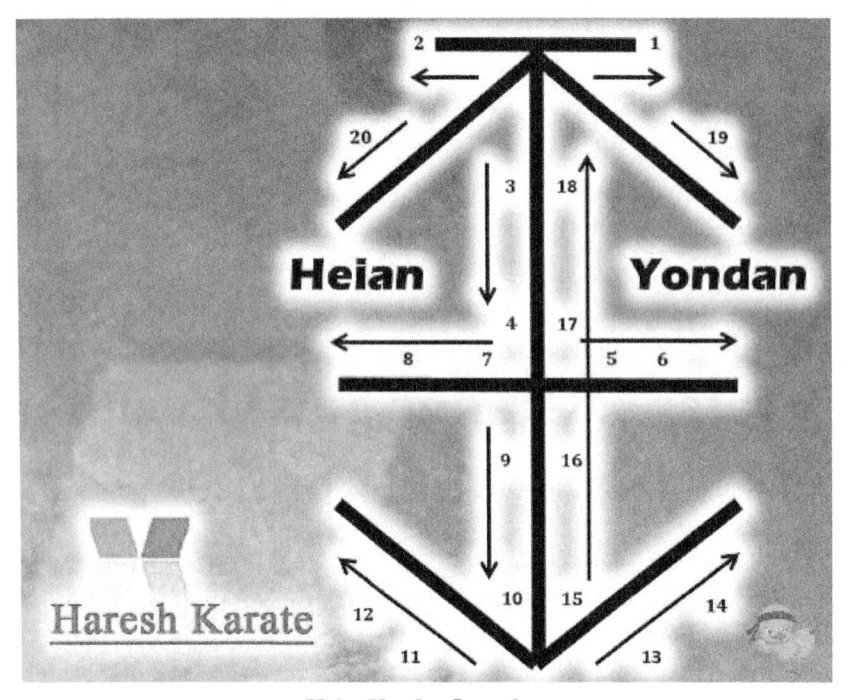

Heian Yondan floor plan.
Haresh karate, CC BY-SA 4.0 <https://creativecommons.org/licenses/by-sa/4.0>, via Wikimedia Commons: https://commons.wikimedia.org/wiki/File:Karate_Kata_Heian_Yondan_Pattern.jpg

One of the critical components of karate is kata, a series of movements practiced in a sequence to simulate a fight against multiple opponents. Heian Yondan Kata is an intermediate-level kata typically learned after practicing the first three Heian katas. This section breaks down the Heian Yondan Kata and provides tips on how to master it.

Understand the Concepts

Before attempting to learn the Heian Yondan Kata, it is crucial to understand its concepts. This kata involves a series of movements simulating fighting against multiple opponents. It includes techniques like blocking, striking, kicking, and shifting positions. Understanding the rhythm of the movements and how they flow together to create a fluid sequence is also essential.

Practice Techniques

First, practicing individual techniques making up the Heian Yondan Kata is essential. Focus on perfecting them before moving on to the next

one to ensure you have a strong foundation before attempting to perform the kata. Some techniques to focus on include:
- **Front Kick:** This primary kick involves kicking with your front foot. Practice maintaining proper form, keeping your balance, and chambering the kicking leg.
- **Downward Block:** This block involves bringing your arm down from the outside to the inside of your body to defend against an overhead strike. Focus on keeping your arm and wrist aligned and your elbow down.
- **Double Punch:** This technique involves punching with both hands simultaneously. Practice maintaining proper form, including aligning your elbows and fists with your shoulders.

Learn the Sequence

Once you have a strong foundation of techniques, it is time to learn the Heian Yondan Kata sequence. Break it into smaller sections and practice each until you can perform it seamlessly. Slowly build up and practice the entire sequence until you can achieve it confidently and fluently. Record yourself practicing so you can identify areas for improvement.

Focus on Breathing

Proper breathing is an essential aspect of karate. When practicing the Heian Yondan Kata, maintain a regular breathing pattern. Inhale deeply before performing a technique, and exhale with each strike or block to maintain rhythm and control your movements. The more stable your breathing, the more fluid and powerful your kata will be.

Practice with Partners

Practicing with partners is essential to mastering techniques and kata in karate. Find a training partner and practice the Heian Yondan Kata together. It will refine your movements and timing and build confidence and endurance. Communicate with your partner to help each other improve.

Mastering the Heian Yondan Kata in karate requires patience, discipline, and dedication. Remember, focus on the concepts, practice individual techniques, learn the sequence, focus on breathing, and practice with partners. With consistent practice and an unwavering commitment, you can master the Heian Yondan Kata in karate.

Heian Godan Kata

Heian Godan

Heian Godan floor plan

The Heian Godan Kata is your next challenge if you are a green belt. This traditional kata requires focus, precision, timing, balance, and coordination. This section provides an overview of the moves and explains their translations to help you master this kata.

Preparation

The first step is to stand at the center of the mat, facing the front of the dojo. Keep your feet shoulder-width apart, arms on your sides. Bow to show respect to the dojo and your sensei. Bring your hands up to your chest and take one step forward with your left foot. This is the starting position for Heian Godan Kata.

Movements

Heian Godan Kata consists of 23 movements, divided into four parts. The first part includes three moves to the left, followed by a right-handed block. The second part moves to the right and consists of a series of strikes and kicks. The third part comprises stepping back and blocking, followed by a spin and a strike. The fourth part includes a series of blocks and punches, ending with a right-handed hammer fist.

Timing

Timing is crucial in karate, and Heian Godan Kata is no exception. Every move must be executed with precision and timeously. Ensure to count the steps and focus on each technique. Don't rush, but don't hesitate, either. Remember to take a deep breath before each move to stay focused, centered, and relaxed.

Visualization

Visualization is a powerful technique to help you improve your karate practice. Before you start the kata, do the following:

1. Visualize yourself performing each move flawlessly.
2. Picture yourself moving fluidly, with perfect timing and technique.
3. Imagine yourself feeling confident, strong, and focused.
4. Visualize yourself succeeding, and it will become a reality.

Practice

Heian Godan Kata requires dedication and effort to master. Repeat the kata several times slowly and gradually increase the speed. Practice with a partner or in front of a mirror to get feedback and improve your technique. Don't be afraid to make mistakes. Instead, learn from them and keep going. If you put in the hard work, you will soon master Heian Godan Kata. Remember to prepare yourself mentally, execute each move precisely, focus on timing, visualize success, and practice consistently. With dedication and effort, you can master Heian Godan

Kata and progress in your karate journey.

Tekki Shodan

Tekki Shodan

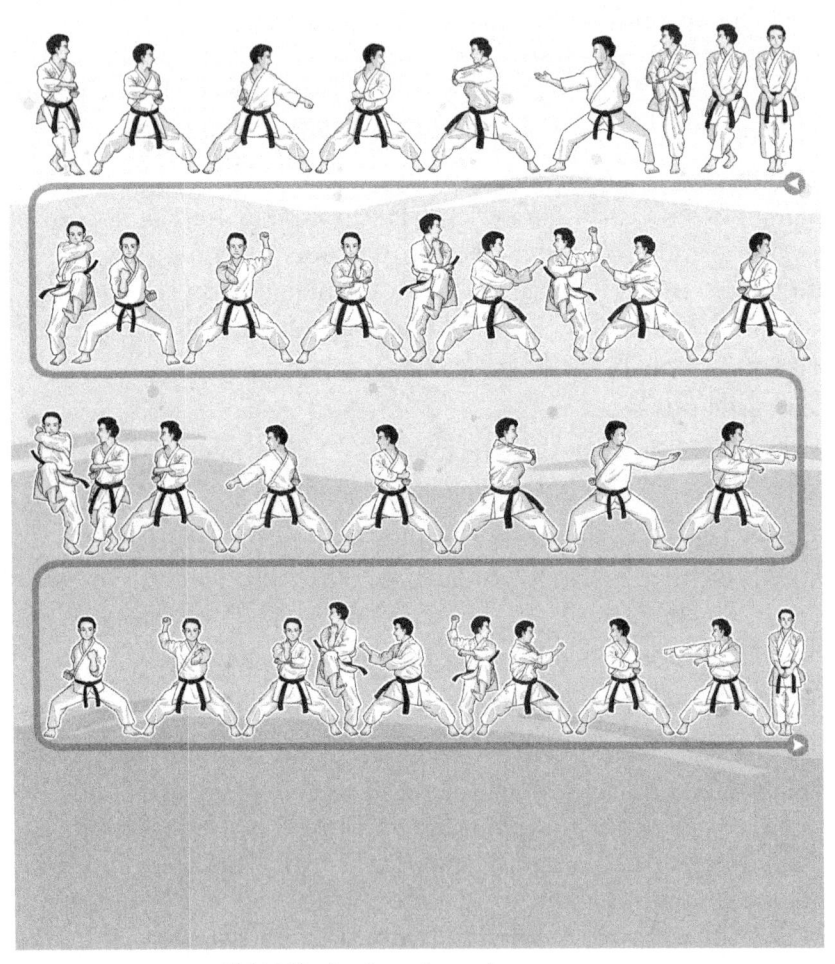

Tekki Shodan floor plan and movements.

A green belt in karate symbolizes you have learned the fundamental concepts in your martial arts journey and are on your way to mastering your techniques. One of the requirements for this rank is mastering the Tekki Shodan Kata. This kata focuses on developing soft, fluid movements to engage with your opponent effectively. The Tekki Shodan Kata is a primary series of sequential actions of stepping in different directions while executing various kicks, punches, and blocks. This section walks you through the Tekki Shodan Kata, highlighting the critical steps necessary to achieve mastery.

Learn the Basic Stance

You must learn the basic stance to execute the Tekki Shodan Kata correctly. Start by standing with your feet together, then move your right foot forward while pivoting on your left foot. Your feet should be shoulder-width apart, with your back foot at a 45-degree angle to maintain balance. The knees should be slightly bent, and the hips should be tucked in, allowing you to transfer your weight between your feet.

Master the First Three Steps

The first three steps in the Tekki Shodan Kata involve a sequence of punches, kicks, and blocks:

1. Punch forward with your right arm, then place your left arm parallel to your stomach while turning your hips.
2. Raise your left leg and pivot on your right foot, executing a front kick.
3. Step forward with your left foot and execute a downward block with your right arm.
4. Perform the same sequence, but this time using your left arm to punch, your right leg to kick, and your left arm to block.

Polish Your Movements

As you continue to practice, focus on your movements. They should be fluid, fast, and powerful. Your punches should land squarely on your imaginary opponent, and your kicks should be quick and secure. Practice moving swiftly and gracefully while maintaining a solid stance.

Internalize the Correct Breathing and Timing

Correct breathing and timing are vital in executing the Tekki Shodan Kata correctly. Inhale sharply as you pull your arm back for a punch, then sharply exhale when you perform a strike. The sound created by your exhalation should be audible and sharp. Appropriately timing the breath will synchronize your movements with your breathing and make more effective strikes.

Practice with Sparring Partners

Take your practice to the next level by testing your skills with a sparring partner. As you practice with a person, you will appreciate the importance of timing, distancing, and precision in your movements. Observe how your partner moves and adjust yourself accordingly. Sparring allows you to develop the right mindset of calmness, focus, and awareness and enhances reflexes.

Mastering the Tekki Shodan Kata is no small feat. It requires dedication, patience, and commitment to detail. However, as you become more fluent with the sequence, your techniques evolve, and your movements become naturally more fluid. Therefore, take your time, practice regularly, and always remember that true mastery is a journey, not a destination. By following the steps outlined above, your journey to becoming a karate Purple Belt will be more enjoyable, rewarding, and, most of all, successful.

Kihon-Ippon Kumite

Kihon-Ippon Kumite is an essential element of karate training with one-step sparring techniques. This section looks closer at Kihon-Ippon Kumite and how to master it. From the basics to the advanced, it explores various approaches and drills to help you become a better martial artist.

Basics

Kihon-Ippon Kumite is a sparring technique performing a pre-determined sequence of moves with a partner. This technique is fundamental in karate because it helps students learn how to react quickly and effectively in various situations. The method is also excellent for improving focus and coordination.

Sequence

Kihon-Ippon Kumite consists of a series of moves divided into two parts. The first part involves the attacker executing an attack, which the defender blocks. The second part consists of the defender counterattacking with a pre-determined sequence of moves. The attacker and defender trade roles after each sequence, allowing both partners to practice their skills.

Sparring With Partner

Starting Kihon-Ippon Kumite with a partner at the same skill level or slightly higher is essential. This ensures that the technique is performed correctly and safely. The partners must wear the appropriate protective gear to protect themselves from injury. Protective equipment includes gloves, mouthguards, and groin protectors.

Form Practice

When practicing Kihon-Ippon Kumite, maintaining a proper stance is vital. The right karate stance is keeping your knees slightly bent, your feet shoulder-width apart, and your weight evenly distributed. Keep your hands up to protect your face, with your elbows close to your sides. Always keep your eyes on your partner. Practice the technique slowly at first and gradually increase the speed and intensity. Pay close attention to your partner and ensure you communicate effectively. Break the process down into small steps and practice each step until it becomes second nature.

Kihon-Ippon Kumite is a crucial element of karate training, helping students learn to react quickly and effectively. It is an excellent technique for improving focus, coordination, and physical strength. Practicing the technique safely and with a partner of the same or slightly higher skill level is essential. Remember to maintain a proper stance, communicate effectively with your partner, and practice the technique in small steps. With time and dedication, you will master this technique and become a skilled karate student.

Tips for Mastering Orange and Green Belt Katas and Kumite

Karate is a martial art emphasizing physical fitness, mental toughness, and discipline. Orange and green belts are significant milestones in this journey, representing intermediate ranks. Mastering katas and kumite at this level can be challenging, but you can achieve your goal with the proper training and guidance. This section shares tips and techniques to improve your orange and green belt katas and kumite.

Practice Daily

Consistency is vital for mastering katas and kumite. Set aside some time each day to practice and stick to it. Focus on at least one or two katas during each session and break down each movement into manageable steps. The same applies to kumite, to practice different moves repetitively until you perfect them. Take your time and don't rush, which can lead to bad habits. Instead, focus on mastering each step before moving on to the next.

Focus on Proper Technique

Ensure you're doing each technique correctly from the start. Focusing on the proper form will help you avoid developing bad habits that are hard to break later on. If you need help executing a particular technique, ask your sensei or watch training videos to learn the correct way. The competition judges look for precision and accuracy, so ensure your techniques are on point. An excellent way to check your technique is by recording yourself and watching it.

Improve Your Fitness Level

Orange and green belts require significant physical fitness. You should have an excellent cardiovascular endurance level, strength, and flexibility. The better your physical fitness, the better you'll be at kata and kumite. Stability, fluidity, and control are essential for success, so ensure you incorporate fitness exercises into your training regimen. Incorporate a mix of strength, endurance, and stretching exercises into your training routine.

Diet and Rest

Proper nutrition and hydration are essential for mastering katas and kumite. Eat healthy meals with the right protein, carbohydrates, and fats. Pay attention to your hydration level, which is significant in performance. Lastly, get enough rest. Having adequate rest between training sessions is vital for your body and mind to recover. A good night's sleep can go a long way in improving your performance.

Weekly Assessments

Take time each week to assess your progress. Track the katas and kumite you learned and any difficulties you encountered. Keep a journal of your progress and use it to set yourself goals for the upcoming week. It will help you stay on track and ensure consistent progress. If you are struggling, ask your sensei for guidance and assistance. With their help, you can keep progressing in the right direction.

Believe In Yourself

One of the essential aspects of mastering katas and kumite is your mental state. Believe in yourself. Don't let fear or self-doubt hold you back. Visualize yourself performing katas and kumite without any mistakes. Set goals and work hard to achieve them. Remember, the mind is as crucial as the body in karate. If you think you can do it, you will.

Mastering orange and green belt katas and kumite in karate can be challenging but achievable with exemplary dedication and guidance. You can reach your goals through consistent practice, focusing on proper technique, improving your fitness, training with a partner, and believing in yourself. Remember, karate is a journey requiring patience, persistence, and hard work. Stay committed to your training, and you'll move up the ranks in no time.

Chapter 6: Purple and Brown Belt Katas

Karate enthusiasts know the journey toward the black belt involves mastering a series of katas, each more intricate than the last. The purple and brown belt katas are no exception. With their complex combinations of punches, kicks, and blocks, these forms challenge even the most seasoned practitioners. However, the key to success lies in discipline and practice. By dedicating themselves to the art and committing fully to each movement, karatekas can unlock a whole new level of skill and precision.

Whether you're striving for a purple or brown belt, the journey toward mastery is exciting and filled with challenges and rewards. This chapter covers four essential katas practiced by purple and brown belts. From the flowing movements of Bassai-Dai to the dynamic Enpi Kata, these katas are crucial for any serious practitioner. This chapter explains, translates, and illustrates the techniques to perform each form. By the end of this chapter, you'll be well on your way to mastering these complex katas and achieving your next belt.

Bassai-Dai

Bassai-Dai floor plan and movements

Bassai-Dai is a Kyokushin kata emphasizing power and speed. It includes several techniques, like strikes, kicks, and blocks. These striking techniques must be performed with passion and precision. The kicks are fast and hard and highlight the importance of balance and agility. The basic movement in Bassai-Dai is the horse stance, which builds lower body strength. The featured techniques in Bassai-Dai enable the students to fight with confidence and power.

The Bassai-Dai Kata is performed in an intimidating stance with arms held high. This form focuses on powerful, swift movements requiring strength and agility. The key to mastering this kata is to move precisely with purpose, directing each punch and kick. This section explains the Bassai-Dai Kata, its translation, and essential techniques to perform this form. By the end of this chapter, you'll better understand what it takes to master the Bassai-Dai Kata and impress your friends and training partners.

Translation

Firstly, let's break down what the Bassai-Dai Kata translates to in English. Bassai-Dai means "to penetrate a fortress," which represents mastering your inner fortress and channeling that strength into practice. This form often symbolizes the strength and discipline to break through any obstacle.

Techniques

The beginning of the kata involves a series of movements aiming to destabilize your opponent by blocking and striking. You need a solid foundation and stable gravity center to perform this effectively. Focus on keeping your feet shoulder-width apart and your knees slightly bent, even as you move through the kata's steps. Use your core muscles to generate power and balance throughout your movements. Keeping a steady and grounded stance is critical.

Next comes the "hinge" technique. This technique involves using your arms to deflect your opponent's attack while simultaneously striking with a counterblow. First, use your hips to pivot sideways away from the attack. Next, keep your feet planted, bend your knees, and use your arms to block. As you block, use your hips to turn back towards your opponent, throwing a punch or strike. This motion should be fluid and snappy.

After the hinge technique, move into several combination movements focusing on taking down your opponent, controlling their limbs, and destabilizing their balance. You must learn moves like the "sweep" and the "hook." The sweep uses your foot to trip your opponent while simultaneously pulling their arm, throwing them off balance. The hooking technique uses your elbow or forearm to strike your opponent's arm or leg, to cause a stumble or fall. These moves require good timing and accuracy.

The Bassai-Dai Kata ends with a series of movements focusing on incapacitating your opponent completely. This involves delivering a final, powerful strike to disable them. To perform this effectively, you must focus on generating power from your legs, through your hips and core, and into your arms. By keeping a solid foundation and using your entire body, you'll deliver an impactful blow leaving your opponent stunned.

Mastering the Bassai-Dai Kata requires power, technique, and precision. You'll take huge strides toward mastering this powerful kata by focusing on your foundation, pivoting technique, destabilization moves, and final strikes. Remember, consistent practice and attention to detail are the keys to success in karate. So, keep at it; soon enough, you'll be a master of the Bassai-Dai Kata.

Kanku-Dai

Kanku Dai

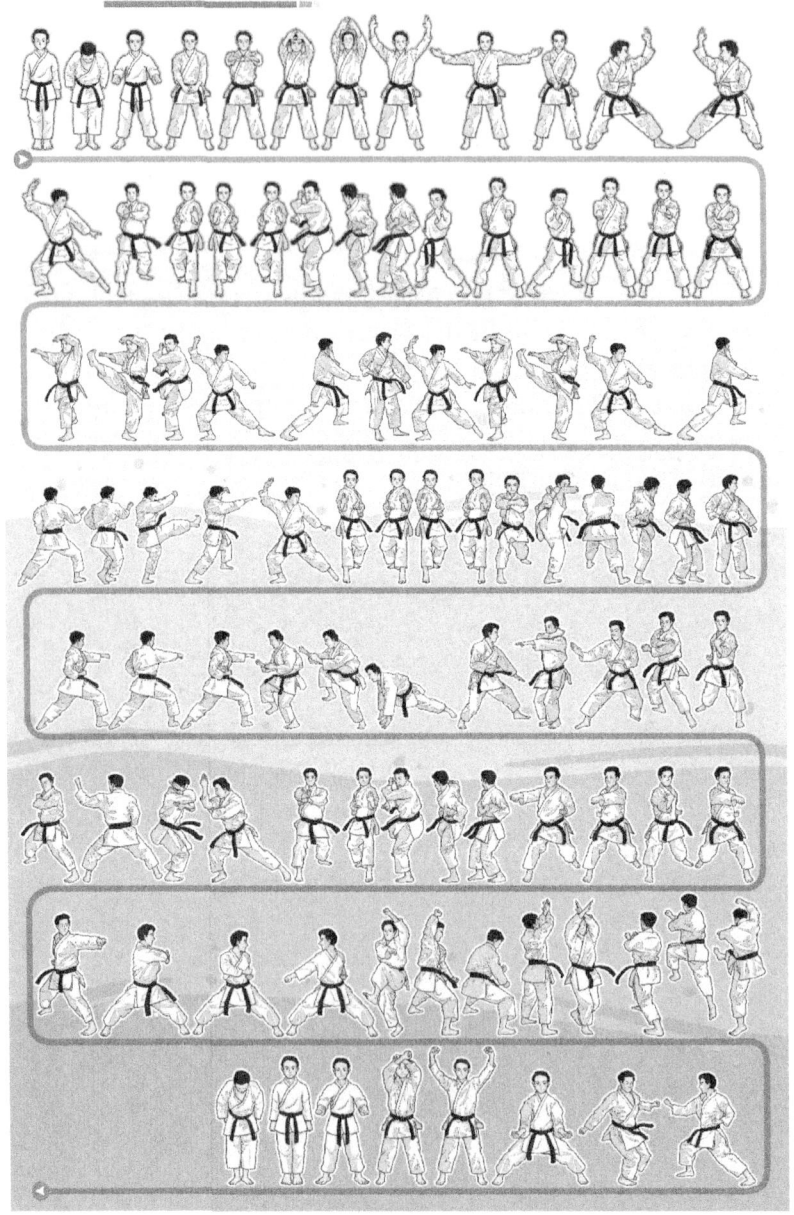

Kanku-dai floor plan and movements

Kanku-Dai Kata is one of the most complex and fascinating karate forms. It develops strong stances, fluid movements, and body alignment precision. With five stances, multiple strikes, and a series of intricate turns, it's no wonder beginners often need help executing it flawlessly. However, with practice and a deep understanding of the techniques, mastering the Kanku-Dai Kata is possible. This section discusses each technique in the kata, providing clear explanations and illustrations to help you perfect your form.

- **Mawashi Geri (Roundhouse Kick):** The Mawashi Geri is a unique kick that involves swinging the leg in a circular motion and striking the target with the ball of the foot. To perform this technique correctly, stand in a left-front stance and lift your right leg. Next, pivot your left foot and kick your right leg at a 45-degree angle. Bring your leg back to the starting position and return to a right front stance. Keep your arms close to the body as you kick, maintaining proper balance throughout.

Mawashi Geri.
Regine Becker, Copyrighted free use, via Wikimedia Commons:
https://commons.wikimedia.org/wiki/File:MaeWashiGeri.jpg

- **Tettsui Uchi (Hammer Fist Strike):** Tettsui Uchi is a crucial technique in the Kanku-Dai Kata as it strikes the opponent's vital points. Starting in a left hip stance, lift both arms to shoulder height. Make a tight fist with your right hand and bring it down in a hammering motion, hitting the opponent with the base of the hand. Maintain eye contact with your target throughout, keeping your left arm extended forward while your right arm strikes.

Tettsui-Uchi

- **Yoko-Geri (Sidekick):** Yoko-Geri is a versatile and powerful technique to attack the opponent's legs or the side of their body. Starting in a left front stance, bring your left leg up, pivoting on your right foot. Next, kick your left leg out to the side, striking your target with the blade of your foot. Return to your starting position and repeat the technique with your other leg. Keep your guard up and your arms close to protect yourself from counterattacks.

Yoko-Geri

- **Morote-Uke (Double-handed Block):** Morote-Uke is a defensive technique that blocks and controls your opponent's arms. To perform this technique, stand in a left front stance, lift your right knee, and bring both hands together in front of your chest. When the opponent attacks, use both arms to block their arms and push them away. Maintain a firm stance and proper balance throughout.

Morote-Uke

- **Gyaku-Zuki (Reverse Punch):** Gyaku-Zuki is a fundamental technique of striking the opponent with a powerful reverse punch. To perform this technique, stand in a left front stance, bend your left elbow, and pull it back toward your body, creating a powerful chain reaction to channel the strength of your entire body to your punching arm. Then, without shifting your stance, bring your right arm forward while twisting your hips, and throw a punch with your right arm. Keep your elbow down and your wrist straight as you punch.

Kanku-Dai is a kata that entails many complex movements, emphasizing speed, focus, and strength. It is a powerful and dynamic karate form demanding excellent balance and control. The kata has an elaborate sequence of moves, including several turning and jumping techniques. It enhances the student's reflexes and hand-eye coordination. This kata provides an excellent opportunity for students to showcase their skills in front of their peers and instructors.

Jion Kata

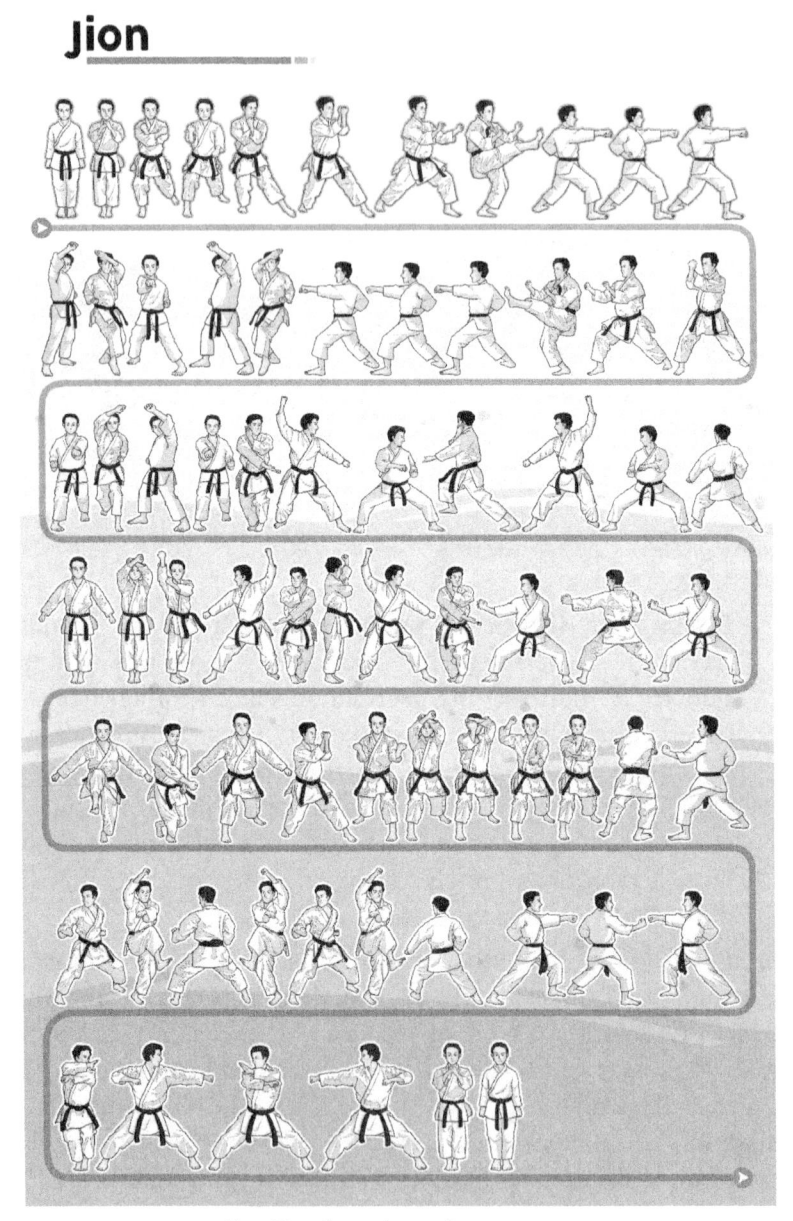

Jion

Jion Kata floor plan and movements.

Jion Kata is a traditional Okinawan kata emphasizing focus, balance, and footwork. It includes several blocking and striking techniques, requiring students to have excellent control. This kata develops the student's timing, helps improve their concentration, and teaches them to adapt to various situations. It is challenging and requires consistency and patience to master.

For karate enthusiasts, mastering the Jion Kata is a significant milestone in their journey to becoming black belts. This kata dates back to the 12th century and is revered for its strong, fast movements simulating a real-life fight. The Jion Kata is a sequence of movements requiring strength, speed, and execution. This section dives deep into the techniques to perform this kata correctly.

- **Front Snap Kick:** The front snap kick is performed at the beginning of the kata and requires executing rapid movements. The technique involves kicking forward with one leg, landing on the same foot, and immediately executing another kick with the other foot. Focusing on the technique's fluidity and speed is crucial while maintaining your balance to pull off this move.
- **Low Block and High Block:** These two moves are frequently combined in one action during the kata sequence. The low block is executed to the left side, followed by a high block towards the right. The technique requires excellent coordination and timing to make the move look smooth.
- **Inside Block and Outside Block:** Similar to the low block and high block combination, the inside and outside block techniques demand precise execution to be effective. The inside block is executed with one hand on the opposite side of the body, while the outer block is performed with both hands on the same side.
- **Elbow Strike:** The elbow strike is one of the most powerful moves in the Jion Kata sequence. The technique requires a rapid and forceful motion, emphasizing the elbow's use to strike and block. You must focus on balance and body movement to execute this move correctly.
- **Knee Strike:** The knee strike is executed toward the end of the kata sequence. The technique requires the swift execution of a knee strike toward your opponent's midsection. The move requires excellent balance and coordination to be effective.

Mastering the Jion Kata techniques requires much practice and patience. Understanding and focusing on the technique's fluidity, strength, and speed is essential. The abovementioned techniques form the foundation to level up your karate game. In all karate disciplines, including Shito Ryu and Shotokan Karate, the Jion Kata is crucial in building mental and physical discipline.

Enpi Kata

Enpi kata floor plan and movements

Enpi Kata, known as the "Flying Swallow Kata," emphasizes mobility, speed, and agility. The kata includes several high kicks and strikes, and the movement is fluid and graceful. This kata improves the student's flexibility, speed, and precision. In addition, it teaches the students how to react quickly and swiftly change direction during a fight.

If you plan to learn the Enpi Kata, you're in for a thrilling ride. This kata is one of the most visually impressive in Shotokan Karate, known for its quick and sharp movements, kicks, punches, and blocks. Enpi Kata is a traditional Japanese martial art that is challenging to master. However, you can perfect this kata with the proper techniques and practice. This section takes you through some essential techniques to perform Enpi Kata successfully.

- **Stepping Technique (Fumikomi):** Enpi Kata's stepping technique is critical for creating momentum and producing power. To perform the Fumikomi technique, take three steps forward with your left foot, extend it firmly, and pull back with your right foot. This movement should create a sound known as Kiai that puts your whole body into the attack.

Fumikomi

- **Elbow Thrust Technique (Empi Uchi):** The elbow thrust technique in Enpi Kata is essential to its arsenal. After taking three steps forward with the Fumikomi technique, twist your body to the left, raising your right arm and elbow. Then thrust your elbow forward, hitting your imaginary opponent's head or throat, and pull back immediately.

Empi Uchi

- **High Block and Kick (Jodan Uke and Mae Geri):** Enpi Kata features many kicking and blocking techniques, including the High Block and Kick combination. To perform this technique, raise your left arm for a Jodan Uke (high block), lift your right knee, and perform a Mae Geri (Front Kick), striking your opponent's face.

Jodan uke

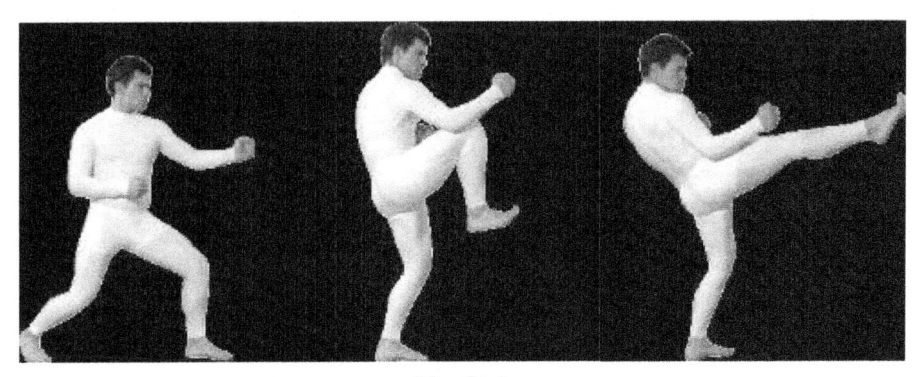

Mae Geri.
User:Evdcoldeportes, CC BY-SA 2.5 CO <https://creativecommons.org/licenses/by-sa/2.5/co/deed.en>, via Wikimedia Commons: https://commons.wikimedia.org/wiki/File:EVD-kumite-119.jpg

- **Reverse Punch (Gyaku Zuki):** The Reverse Punch (Gyaku Zuki) is a fundamental technique in Shotokan karate and a crucial component in Enpi Kata. To execute the Reverse Punch, chamber your right hand by your hip, step forward with your left foot, pivot your left foot, and push your right fist toward your opponent's face.

- **Jumping and Spinning (Tobi and Kaiten):** Enpi Kata ends with a series of dynamic moves, including jumping and spinning. To perform the Tobi (jump), crouch down, propel yourself off the ground by extending your legs, and land back into your Kiba-dachi stance. As for Kaiten (spinning), rotate your body and strike your imaginary opponent in mid-air.

Enpi Kata is not easy to master, but practicing these essential techniques means you're on your way to becoming a pro. Remember, consistent and persistent training is the key to success. We hope these techniques provide insight to help hone your skills. Whether a beginner or an advanced karateka, these techniques suit anyone looking to improve their Enpi Kata.

The purple and brown belt katas, including Bassai-Dai, Kanku-Dai, Jion Kata, and Enpi Kata, are vital to developing a student's skills and proficiency. These katas help students improve their agility, speed, power, and concentration. In addition, they emphasize the importance of self-discipline, patience, and mental focus, crucial attributes a karate student should possess. So, if you are a purple or brown belt karate student, perfect these katas.

Chapter 7: Brown and Black Belt Kumites

The practice of kumite, or sparring, is a crucial component of martial arts training. For karatekas aiming for black belt, brown and black belt kumites are essential to the process. Once they have perfected the kumite basics, practitioners can move on to semi-free sparring (Jiyu Ippon Kumite) and free sparring (Jiyu Kumite). While the two have similarities, there are critical differences between them.

This chapter outlines the main features, techniques, and steps of Jiyu Ippon Kumite and Jiyu Kumite. Understanding these drills is essential as they are significant to brown and black belt practice. The knowledge acquired here will help karatekas perform these drills to the best of their ability. Mastering these kumites is essential before progressing to the next level. Read on to learn more about brown and black belt kumite.

Brown and black belts use sparring.
https://www.pexels.com/photo/men-doing-martial-arts-8611418/

Brown and Black Belt Kumites

Brown and black belt kumites test endurance, strategy, and skill. It involves full-contact sparring with an opponent of the same skill level or higher. The karateka must demonstrate their mastery of techniques, such as blocks, strikes, and kicks. The objective is not to knock out the opponent but to score points through proper execution of techniques.

Timing

One key component of brown and black belt kumites is timing. A split second can make all the difference in winning or losing. Karatekas must demonstrate effective distancing to control the distance between them and their opponent. Footwork is crucial to move quickly and evade an opponent's attack.

Control

Control is another crucial aspect that should be considered during brown and black belt kumites. Karatekas must strike their opponent with enough force to score a point but not enough to injure them. They must use control in their defense, being aware of their opponent's movements and anticipating their attacks. It requires physical mastery and mental focus, and sharpness.

Character

Brown and black belt kumites test a karateka's character - respect for their opponent, following rules and regulations, and demonstrating humility in victory and defeat. Karatekas must show perseverance in improving their skills and techniques. These are essential qualities a true martial artist must possess. The ability to control emotions and stay focused are vital traits to develop.

Courage

Lastly, brown and black belt kumites allow karateka to test their limits and face their fears. It takes a lot of courage to go against a skilled opponent and risk being hit. Failing in a brown or black belt kumite seems discouraging, but it's an opportunity to reflect on what went wrong and to improve. In the end, karatekas emerge more potent and confident in their abilities.

Brown and black belt kumites are more than sparring with an opponent. They test a karateka's physical and mental abilities, courage, and character. It's about something other than winning or losing but about each karateka honing what they've learned in training to demonstrate their skill, intelligence, and control. Brown and black belt kumites push karatekas to their limits, but they become more robust, disciplined, and resilient.

Jiyu Ippon Kumite (Semi-Free Sparring)

Jiyu Ippon Kumite, known as semi-free sparring, is a popular method in traditional karate training. It is one of the most challenging yet satisfying exercise forms helping practitioners improve their technique and sparring skills. In addition, Jiyu Ippon Kumite allows karatekas to showcase their agility, timing, and precision skills. This section explores the main features, techniques, and steps to master Jiyu Ippon Kumite.

Main Features

Jiyu Ippon Kumite is a combination of technique and sparring. Practitioners are allowed to use any methods provided they are controlled and do not cause harm to their opponents. During Jiyu Ippon Kumite, there is no pre-planned attack sequence, and the opponent moves spontaneously to attack or counterattack. This training incorporates speed and distance management, allowing practitioners to perfect footwork and body coordination.

Techniques Used

Jiyu Ippon Kumite allows practitioners to apply techniques in a controlled but more realistic environment. A masterful Jiyu Ippon Kumite requires knowing and executing basic techniques on the spot. Here are the most effective techniques in Jiyu Ippon Kumite and pointers on improving your technique.

- **Use Your Footwork to Your Advantage:** Footwork is crucial in Jiyu Ippon Kumite. Moving your feet quickly and efficiently to outmaneuver your opponent is essential. One tip is to practice moving in all directions and dodging to avoid being hit. You can quickly step in or out of striking range, making it difficult for your opponent to land a clean hit.

- **Focus on Blocking:** Effective blocking is essential in Jiyu Ippon Kumite. Practicing blocking with precision and using your hands and arms to protect your vital areas is necessary. One technique is to block to the outside of your opponent's strike, known as Uke. You can use kicks to block strikes. Blocking immediately once your opponent initiates a move is crucial.

- **Apply Counterattacks:** Counterattacks are significant in Jiyu Ippon Kumite. Once you block your opponent's strike, you can strike back. Some techniques include Jodan, a punch to the head, and Chudan, a punch to the torso. You can also use kicks and sweeps to take your opponent off balance. It is essential to ensure your counterattacks are precise and controlled.

- **Take Advantage of Distractions:** Distractions are effective for catching your opponent off guard and creating an opportunity to attack. Some techniques include Feints – faking a move to deceive your opponent, and Moving Targets - moving your head or body to make it harder to hit. By using these techniques, you create openings to strike your opponent.

- **Stay Focused and Calm:** Lastly, staying focused and calm is critical to mastering Jiyu Ippon Kumite. Maintaining a clear and focused mindset is essential, even when under pressure. Avoid becoming agitated and losing your cool, which leads to mistakes. By staying focused, you anticipate your opponent's moves and react accordingly.

Steps of Jiyu Ippon Kumite

The steps to practice Jiyu Ippon Kumite vary from dojo to dojo, but the basics remain the same.

1. Firstly, start with a thorough warm-up session to avoid injuries.
2. Face your opponent and bow to begin the sparring session.
3. Decide who will be the attacker and who will be the defender.
4. The attacker decides which technique to use while the defender performs a block, then quickly follows up with a counter-technique.
5. Stay relaxed, manage your distance, and maintain good footwork during sparring.
6. Lastly, bow to your opponent to indicate the end of the session.

Jiyu Ippon Kumite is an excellent training mechanism for improving your karate skills. It tests your technique and sparring abilities and helps build confidence. You can master this karate form and develop essential skills such as agility, timing, and precision with regular practice. The techniques are vast and allow for endless creativity. The key is to stay relaxed and focused and maintain good footwork during sparring. Regularly practice Jiyu Ippon Kumite and see how it enhances your karate skills.

Jiyu Kumite (Free Sparring)

Martial arts are more than just learning forms and techniques. It's about testing yourself physically and mentally against others. For karate practitioners, Jiyu Kumite allows them to show off their skills and learn from their mistakes. Jiyu Kumite, known as free sparring, is crucial in traditional karate training. This section dives into Jiyu Kumite's main features, techniques, and steps of this dynamic and exciting practice.

Main Features

Jiyu Kumite is a sparring practice teaching students how to react quickly and effectively to different fighting styles. Unlike predetermined kumite, Jiyu Kumite doesn't rely on choreographed moves. Instead, students must create their attacks and defenses on the spot. This approach helps practitioners develop thinking on their feet and adapt to changing situations. Additionally, Jiyu Kumite emphasizes the importance of control and respect toward your opponent, keeping both martial artists safe during the sparring session.

Techniques Used

Jiyu Kumite is one of the most exciting and challenging aspects of karate training. Like a real fight, it requires quick reflexes, strategic thinking, and adapting to any situation. In Jiyu Kumite, you must be prepared to work with a wide range of attack techniques, from punches to kicks to elbow strikes.

Firstly, punches (tsuki) are a fundamental technique in Jiyu Kumite. Keeping your guard up is one of the most important things to remember when throwing a punch when sparring. Your opponent will look for weaknesses in your defense, so keep your hands up to protect your face and body. Aim for the chin, solar plexus, or ribs when throwing a punch. Use your whole body, not just your arm, to generate power.

Elbow strikes (empi) are another crucial technique in Jiyu Kumite. Elbow strikes can be used in close-range combat and are incredibly effective when thrown correctly. To throw an elbow strike, bring your elbow up and to the side of your body, then drive it forward using your whole body. The target for an elbow strike will typically be the temple, jaw, or collarbone. Elbow strikes are powerful and can stun or incapacitate an opponent quickly.

Knife-hand strikes (shuto) are commonly used in Jiyu Kumite. Shuto strikes involve striking with the side of your hand and are used in various ways. For example, you can use a shuto strike to the neck or temple to stun your opponent or hit the ribs to knock the wind out of them. To execute a shuto strike, keep your fingers together and your thumb tucked in, then strike with the fleshy part of your hand.

Kicks are essential in Jiyu Kumite and include three main techniques: front kicks (mae geri), side kicks (yoko geri), and roundhouse kicks (mawashi geri). Front kicks are powerful and can keep your opponent at bay. When throwing a front kick, aim for the solar plexus or chin. Side kicks are helpful when your opponent moves laterally and can be delivered to the ribs or knee. Roundhouse kicks are powerful but slower than other kicks. They target the side of the head or the ribs.

Steps of Jiyu Kumite

Before the sparring session, students must warm up and stretch properly. Then, typically perform predetermined exercises to refine their skills and techniques. Once the sparring session starts, there are a few key steps to know.

1. Start with a bow and assume a fighting stance.
2. Test each other with light jabs or footwork before exchanging more advanced techniques.
3. Be aware of your distance and positioning when engaging with your opponent.
4. Use different techniques to attack, defend, and counterattack.
5. Be aware of your opponent's position, movements, and their reactions to your attacks.
6. Use light contact and remain in control at all times.
7. Be respectful of your opponent and their skills.
8. When the bout is finished, bow and shake hands.

Jiyu Ippon Kumite is the second sparring drill practiced by brown and black belts. This sparring is more structured than Jiyu Kumite and follows a predetermined sequence of attacks and blocks. In this drill, students practice prearranged techniques from an offensive and defensive perspective to score points. The methods in this drill include punches, kicks, elbow strikes, and knife-hand strikes.

Jiyu-Ippon and Jiyu Kumite are essential for mastering karate and developing critical martial arts skills, such as focus, balance, precision, and respect. In addition, these kumites help build self-confidence and decision-making abilities, making them valuable practice in the physical and mental aspects of karate. Whether a beginner or an experienced martial artist, these kumites provide an interesting and exciting challenge to take your karate skills to the next level.

Chapter 8: Black Belt Katas I

Take your martial art skills to the next level with advanced black belt katas. These intricate forms are not for the faint-hearted but for those willing to put in the time and effort. The Jitte brings sharp, precise movements to keep your opponent guessing. Tekki Nidan and Tekki Sandan provide a challenge with their focus on strength and balance. The Bassai-sho emphasizes power and speed, always keeping you on your toes.

As a black belt, these katas are the ultimate test of your abilities and showcase your dedication to the craft. This chapter helps you take on the challenge and add these impressive forms to your martial arts arsenal. It covers each kata's meaning, techniques, steps, timing, and tips. You'll be ready to confidently take on the advanced black belt katas by the end.

Jitte Kata

Jitte

Jitte floor plan and movements

Karate is about throwing kicks and punches and encompasses artistic movements called katas. Kata is a sequence of actions mimicking a fight against an imaginary opponent. One of the katas every black belt karateka should learn is the Jitte Kata. Unfortunately, this kata is a hidden gem only a few can perform correctly. This section guides you through learning to perform the Jitte Kata correctly.

Meaning

Jitte means ten hands in Japanese. The purpose of the kata is to show that with proper technique and timing, the karateka can defend against ten opponents. The Jitte Kata helps improve your balance, focus, and coordination. It teaches awareness of your surroundings and uses combat strategies.

Techniques and Steps

The Jitte Kata consists of 24 movements divided into two parts. The first part contains ten moves involving blocking techniques, while the second includes fourteen actions involving striking techniques.

1. Start in a left stance, with fists and open hands on the hips.
2. Step to the right in a horse stance and simultaneously execute a down block (Gedan Barai).
3. Step forward with the front foot and execute a middle inner block (uchi uke) while pivoting on the back foot, ready for a front kick (mae geri).
4. Step forward with the back foot and execute the front kick (mae geri).
5. Land and pull back the front foot and perform a downward middle block (Chudan Gedan Barai).
6. Feint with the front hand and employ a lower-level modified spear-hand strike to the groin (Nage-Azuki).
7. Without retracting the modified spear hand, pivot 270 degrees clockwise.
8. Shift to a front stance and execute a rising block (age uke).
9. Step forward with the back foot and execute a front kick (mae geri).
10. Land and pull back the front foot and perform a middle inner block (uchi uke).
11. Slide the left foot in and raise the right foot to perform a left front kick.

The second part involves striking techniques and has fourteen movements. Like the first part, all the movements require excellent footwork, balance, and coordination.

Timing

The Jitte Kata requires precision and timing. Each move is a response to an attack from an imaginary opponent. Therefore, it's essential to clearly understand the sequence of movements before practicing the kata. Practice each step methodically and ensure each movement flows smoothly to the next. When practicing, please observe your breathing and ensure it syncs with your actions.

Tips

- Practicing with a partner helps you understand the timing and flow of the movements.
- Understanding the meaning behind this kata helps you perform it with the proper perspective.
- Focus on your stance. Ensure it is solid and your hips and shoulders are aligned.
- Consistency is vital to mastery. Practice regularly and aim to improve in every session.

The Jitte Kata is a vital kata every karateka should learn. Learning and mastering the kata requires dedication, practice, and patience. However, when performed correctly, the kata shows your coordination, balance, and focus. If you follow the guidelines in this section, you can complete the Jitte Kata quickly and confidently.

Tekki Nidan Kata

Tekki Nidan (Ne2)

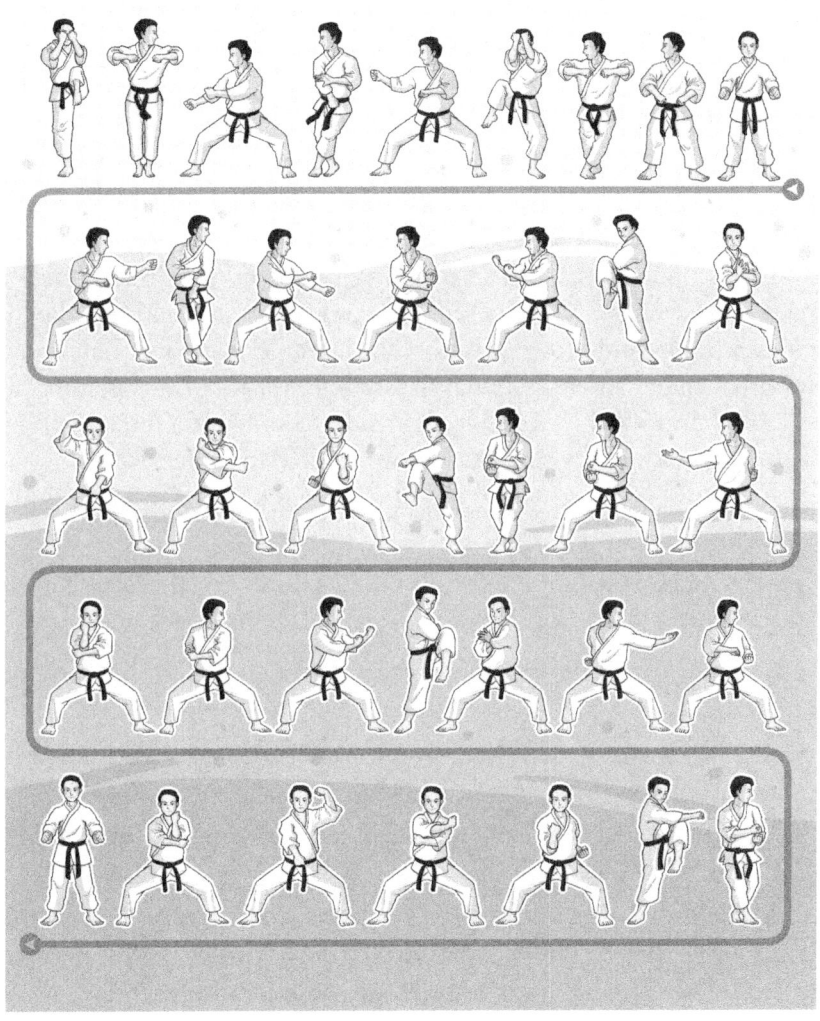

Tekki Nidan floor plan and movements

Kata is the cornerstone of traditional karate practice, and Tekki Nidan is one of the most important and popular forms. A kata is a series of pre-arranged movements and techniques simulating a self-defense situation, and Tekki Nidan Kata is considered one of the most advanced forms.

This ancient kata is a foundation kata, excellent for students to learn and perfect. This section explores the meaning, techniques, timing, and tips for performing Tekki Nidan Kata.

Meaning

Tekki Nidan, known as Naihanchi Nidan, is a powerful and dynamic kata to simulate close-quarter fighting. Its name comes from the Japanese word "Tekki," meaning "iron horse," and "Nidan," meaning "2nd level" or "second step." In this kata, you move linearly, firmly planted on the ground like an "iron horse." Tekki Nidan Kata develops strong leg muscles, improves balance, and develops a proper fighting mindset.

Techniques and Steps

Tekki Nidan Kata comprises 24 movements that must be performed with precise execution. The movements include low stances, punches, blocks, kicks, and twists. The kata moves linearly, with many turns and changes in direction. The techniques and steps in Tekki Nidan Kata develop upper and lower body strength, enhancing balance and promoting agility. Some essential techniques for this kata include Shuto Uke (knife-hand block), Soto-Uke (outside block), and Gedan-Barai (low sweep). Here's a step-by-step breakdown of Tekki Nidan Kata:

1. Begin in a natural stance and perform a Shuto Uke, then pivot and perform a Soto-Uke.
2. Step forward with the left foot into a side stance (Jodan Uke).
3. Perform a right punch and take a front stance (Chudan Uke).
4. Step back with the left foot and perform an inward block (Gedan-Barai).
5. Step forward with the right foot into a front stance and perform an inward elbow strike (Empi-Uchi).
6. Step back with the left foot and perform a low block (Gedan-Barai).
7. Move forward in a low stance with the right foot while performing an inward block (Gedan-Barai).
8. Step forward with the left foot and perform a Shuto-Uke.
9. Step back with the left and perform a low block (Gedan-Barai).
10. Step to the left and perform an outward block (Soto-Uke).
11. Step forward with the right foot into a side stance and perform a front punch.

12. Step forward with the left foot into a natural stance and perform a Shuto-Uke.

Timing

Timing is crucial when performing Tekki Nidan Kata. The timing of your movements must be precise and well-coordinated to simulate an actual self-defense situation. Perform this kata at a slow, controlled pace until you've mastered the techniques and movements. Once you feel comfortable with the kata, increase your speed. The kata should be performed with constant motion, with no pauses between movements.

Tips

To perform Tekki Nidan Kata effectively, keep these tips in mind:

1. Maintain a low gravity center throughout the kata to help you balance and keep your movements grounded.
2. Keep your eyes focused on your opponent while performing the kata.
3. Breathe properly and continuously throughout the kata to maintain physical and mental stamina.
4. Practice the kata repetitively until your movements become fluid and aggressive.
5. Learn to control your body and actions to execute each technique with precision and strength.

Tekki Nidan Kata is an explosive and challenging kata that takes time and dedication to master. You must develop flexibility, strength, and endurance to perfect this kata. While Tekki Nidan Kata appears simple at first glance, it is a complex form requiring advanced techniques and precise timing. However, you can learn to perform this dynamic kata like a true martial artist with consistent practice and dedication. So, take your time, stay focused, and enjoy the journey as you unlock the techniques and timing of this ancient kata.

Tekki Sandan Kata

Tekki Sandan

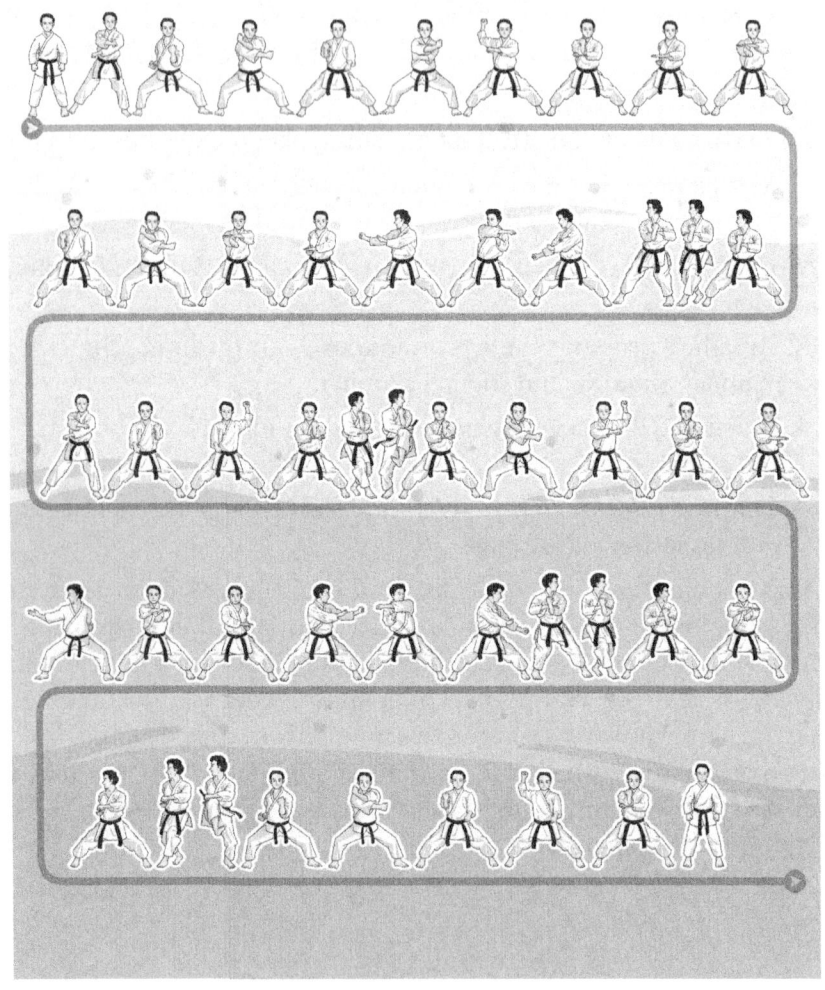

Tekki Sandan floor plan and movements

The Tekki Sandan Kata is a basic form taught after you've attained a blue belt. This section covers the meaning of Tekki Sandan Kata, the techniques, steps, timing, and tips to help you master this kata.

Meaning

Tekki Sandan Kata translates to "Iron Horse Three." It's an excellent representation of the movements and stances while executing the kata. The symbolic importance derives from the firmness of the horse and balance. The balance between the front and back of the feet must be precise, where both feet point in perpendicular directions and provide a stable foundation.

Techniques and Steps

The Tekki Sandan Kata involves fundamental techniques crucial to mastering martial arts. One of the more central techniques includes the "Shuto Uke" technique or the knife hand block. Other moves in this kata are the palm heel strike, punch, and front kick. The kata is quite complex in its stepping techniques and requires moving your legs laterally continually. Remember, practice makes perfect. Start with getting the footwork correct and then work on mastering the various techniques involved.

Timing

Timing is everything in martial arts. For Tekki Sandan Kata, the movements are fast-paced and quite intricate. However, to the untrained eye, they can appear slow. The kata comprises 26 movements and requires roughly 50 seconds to complete. The trick is to move at a consistent speed and ensure every action is in sync.

Tips

1. Focus on your breathing. Remember to inhale and exhale during the movements.
2. Pay attention to your posture and ensure it's correct. An improper posture could cause imbalance.
3. Ensure each movement is precise. It will take time to get it right, but you'll get there with practice.

Your stances must be rooted and stable. The technique becomes effortless when your stances are correct.

Learning the Tekki Sandan Kata will lay a solid foundation for mastering martial arts. First, it's essential to understand the meaning behind the kata, the techniques and steps involved, the timing, and to read the tips to help you master it. Then, you'll execute the kata effortlessly with regular practice, determination, and patience.

Bassai-Sho Kata

Bassai-Sho

Bassai-Sho floor plan and movements.

Bassai-Sho Kata is a martial arts form that originated in Okinawa, Japan. This traditional karate form is widely practiced by martial artists worldwide – and for a good reason. Bassai-Sho Kata embodies agility, power, control, and challenges body and mind. This section explains everything about this dynamic karate form, including its meaning, techniques, timing, and tips on improving your skill.

Meaning

"Bassai-Sho" means "to penetrate a fortress" in Japanese. The art of Bassai-Sho Kata is based upon the two concepts of infiltration and evasion. The movements of Bassai-Sho Kata enable a martial artist to overcome an opponent by making direct, consequential, and effective strikes. The basic principles of Bassai-Sho Kata include mastering footwork, proper alignment, and focus on breathing.

Techniques and Steps

Several techniques and steps are involved in performing Bassai-Sho Kata. However, the most essential include movements, such as:

1. **Hachiji-Dachi:** This stance forms a base for many movements in Bassai-Sho Kata.
2. **Chudan-Uke:** This is a middle block using your forearm to block an attack aimed at your torso.
3. **Age-Uke:** This rising block uses your arm to deflect attacks on your face.
4. **Kiba-Dachi:** This stance is for counterattacks, striking your opponent's legs.
5. **Empi-Uchi:** This is a powerful elbow strike to hit an opponent at close range.

Timing

Timing is an essential component of Bassai-Sho Kata. The art involves grasping the right moment to attack or defend against an opponent. Timing involves recognizing the suitable openings to execute a move, translating to heightened accuracy and precision. The key to timing is controlling your body's movements to avoid telegraphing your next move. Proper alignment, footwork, and breathing are crucial to timing in Bassai-Sho Kata.

Tips

- **Practice Regularly:** Like any martial art form, continued training of Bassai-Sho Kata ensures mastery. In addition, regular practice helps you become more comfortable with the moves and techniques to enhance your skills.

- **Strengthen Your Core:** Core strength is critical in executing Bassai-Sho Kata movements. Strengthen your core through exercises like sit-ups and planks.
- **Seek Feedback:** Your movements are as good as your ability to execute them in karate. Seek feedback from your sensei or peers to understand areas needing improvement.
- **Focus on Breathing:** Karate masters emphasize the importance of controlled breathing during practice. Focus on steady and deep breathing as you execute moves.

Learning Bassai-Sho Kata takes time, effort, and dedication. It requires constant practice, discipline, and focus on mastering the movements and techniques. However, you can achieve great rewards in physical fitness and mental strength with patience and persistence. Whether learning for sport or self-defense, Bassai-Sho Kata is an excellent addition to your martial arts repertoire. Always remember the critical components of Bassai-Sho Kata, including the meaning, techniques, timing, and tips, as they form the foundation of your growth in this beautiful martial arts form.

The black belt katas are an advanced traditional karate form. This chapter covered the meaning, techniques, steps, and timing of the most popular katas among advanced practitioners. With practice, discipline, and focus, you can acquire the skills necessary to clear the fortress of these katas and grow in strength, agility, and mental clarity. Remember, seek feedback when necessary, focus on controlled breathing as you practice, and strengthen your core to increase stability.

Chapter 9: Black Belt Katas II

The Black Belt Katas are a vital aspect of any martial artist's training regimen in karate. From Kanku-Sho to Gankaku, each form has unique challenges testing a practitioner's strength, agility, and mental focus. For example, Hangetsu emphasizes the importance of balance and breath control. Sochin challenges even the most skilled fighters with intricate hand movements and precise footwork. Whether a beginner or a seasoned pro, mastering these katas requires dedication and commitment. But nothing beats the feeling of executing each movement with precision and grace.

This chapter is dedicated to the four black belt katas, providing detailed descriptions. It covers the translation and meaning of each kata, outlines the movements, and offers valuable tips for mastering them. By this chapter's end, you'll understand the four katas and be well on your way to becoming a black belt. The journey is long, but the rewards are great.

Kanku-Sho

Kanku-Sho

Kanku-Sho floor plan and movements

Karate is a dynamic martial art requiring discipline, focus, and continuous practice. Like any martial art, it has its own katas or choreographed patterns of movements. One of these katas is the Kanku-Sho Kata, a second-level kata known for its intricate movements and symbolisms. This section explores the translation, meaning, and significance of Kanku-Sho Kata. Additionally, are tips to help you master this unique kata.

Meaning

Kanku-Sho Kata means "to look at the sky and beckon." This name is derived from one of the movements in the kata where the practitioner performs an upward block with one hand while the other is extended upward as if beckoning or calling forth something from the heavens. This action is believed to represent a moment of meditation where the practitioner takes a moment to reflect and connect with the universe. Most practitioners believe this Kata symbolizes the journey to enlightenment. It's a powerful reminder that with dedication and focus, anything is possible.

Movements

The Kanku-Sho Kata consists of 27 movements divided into three parts: the opening, the middle, and the closing. Each element has its actions and meanings. Initially, the practitioner performs a series of defensive and offensive movements symbolizing the need to protect from external threats. The middle part focuses on slow, deliberate movements emphasizing balance, control, and concentration. The closing part includes finishing moves to end the kata with power and grace. While executing each movement, the practitioner must remain focused and aware of their surroundings.

Tips

To master the Kanku-Sho Kata, start by memorizing the movements and their meanings. Practice each movement slowly and deliberately, focusing on form, stance, and breathing. Once you have memorized the movements, practice performing them with fluidity and grace, keeping your actions precise and controlled, and always maintaining eye contact with your imaginary opponent. Regularly practice the kata to increase your stamina and endurance. The more you practice, the better your execution will become.

Kanku-Sho Kata is a fascinating and profound kata requiring discipline, focus, and practice. Its movements and symbolisms represent the essence of karate, which is the pursuit of physical and spiritual perfection. Mastering this kata teaches you to defend yourself and develop a deeper connection with the universe. So, keep practicing, stay focused, and always remember to look at the sky and beckon.

Hangetsu

Hangetsu

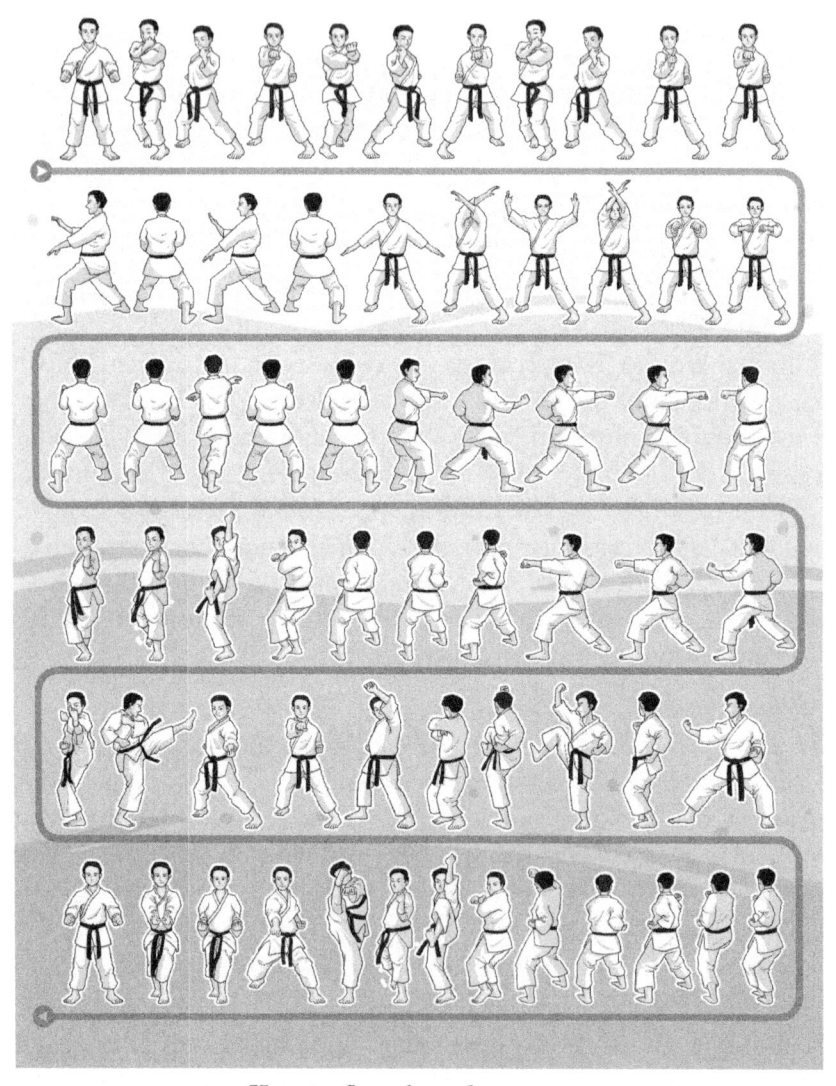

Hangetsu floor plan and movements

For karate enthusiasts, the Hangetsu Kata is a form that must be noticed. This particular kata is one of the most unique and challenging. Hangetsu translates to half-moon, symbolizing the balance between Japanese and Chinese martial arts. This kata is an excellent tool for honing mental focus, physical balance, and precision. This section explores the meaning and movements of Hangetsu Kata and provides tips on how to master it.

Meaning

Hangetsu Kata combines two forms, Gojushiho and Sanchin Kata. The half-moon symbolizes the balance between the physical body and the mind, external martial arts, and internal energy art. The core idea behind this kata is to develop inner strength, speed, and sharp movements. It emphasizes deep, stable stances increasing balance and stability while performing motions redirecting or neutralizing an opponent's attack. The end of this kata is marked by a stance symbolizing the moon at its fullest with both hands held up and palms open.

Movements

This kata is performed slowly and precisely, making it one of the toughest to master. It requires a lot of control and balanced weight to execute each movement correctly. Hangetsu Kata has many circular motions, blocks, strikes, and kicks. It opens with a slow Neko ashi dachi, known as a cat stance, preparing you for the following steady movements. The sequence includes a breathing exercise focusing on relaxing your body while maintaining a constant flow of energy.

Tips

You must have a fundamental understanding and body control of basic stances to master the Hangetsu Kata. It is essential to take things slowly, even slower than usual, and focus on executing each movement with perfect balance. Please pay attention to each movement and understand how it connects to the next one. Also, control your breathing, as this kata requires precision and attention to detail. Another critical aspect to consider is your footwork. Ensure you're grounded and your feet are correctly positioned to avoid losing balance.

The Hangetsu Kata is one of the primary karate forms helping martial artists to unlock their inner strength and achieve balance in their physical and mental state. Its complex movements and emphasis on the balance of mind and body offer a unique opportunity to develop your power, precision, and overall martial art skills. So, try it out and experience the joy of mastering this challenging but rewarding kata. Remember to take things slow, maintain proper breathing techniques, focus on your movements, and keep your feet grounded.

Gankaku

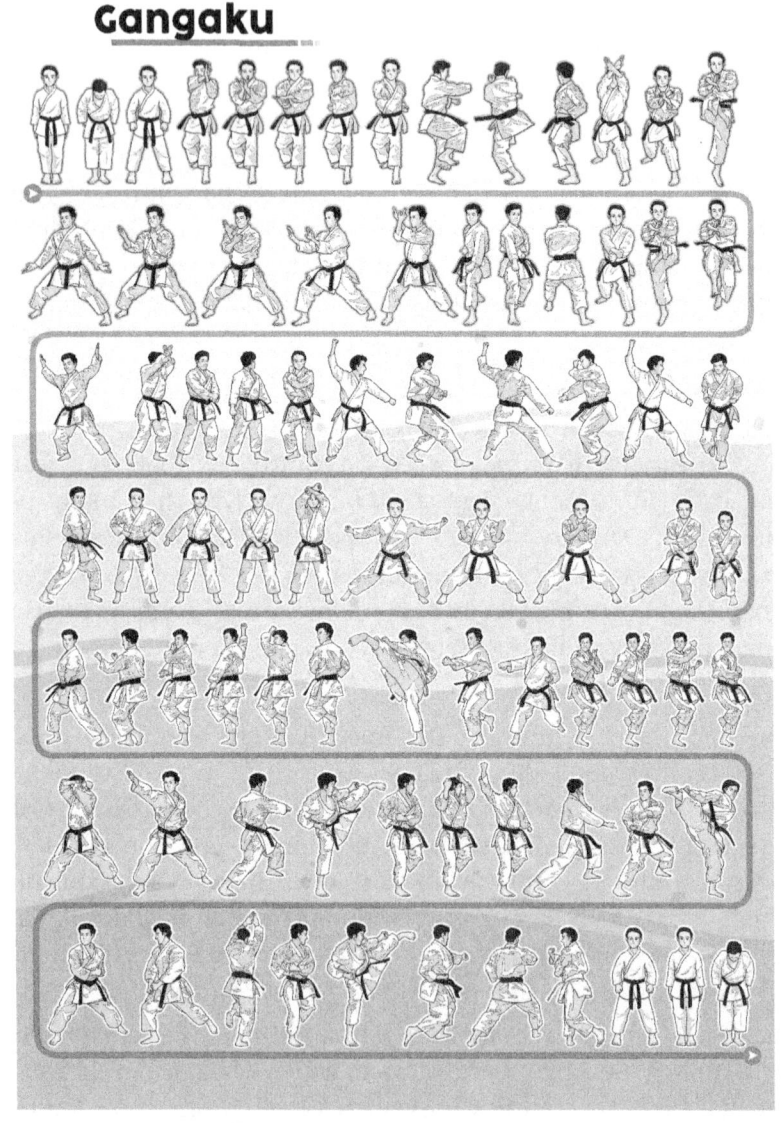

Gankaku floor plan and movements

Karate, a martial art that originated in Okinawa, Japan, has a wide range of kata (forms) with different techniques and movements. One is the Gankaku Kata, known as the "crane on a rock" Kata. This kata uniquely combines stances, kicks, strikes, and blocks and is known for its fluid movements and grace. This section delves deeper into the Gankaku Kata and explores its meaning, movements, and tips.

Meaning

Gankaku Kata, known as Chinto Kata, translates to "crane on a rock" or "fighting on a rock." It is believed to have originated from Chinese martial arts and was brought to Okinawa by a Chinese martial artist named Chintō. The kata is named after a small island near China with rocky terrain, resembling the crane on a rock position. The kata incorporates a crane's movements, symbolizing longevity, grace, and balance, and is considered one of the most beautiful katas in karate.

Movements

The Gankaku Kata contains 42 movements, which include various kicks, strikes, and blocks. The kata starts with a soft and relaxed stance, followed by the "crane on a rock" move, including a crane stance on one leg with the other raised in a front kick position. The kata progresses with stances of various heights, including high kicks, knee strikes, and elbow strikes. It also features hand strikes and a unique move called Koko - the "bird beak" technique to control an opponent's arm. The kata finishes with a "butterfly" kick, where the feet are crossed mid-air, followed by the "crane on a rock" pose.

Tips

Mastering the Gankaku Kata takes time, effort, and practice. Here are some tips to help you perform the kata better:

- Focus on the balance and precision of each movement. For example, the crane stance and front kick require good balance and coordination.
- Focus on your breathing. Deep, controlled breathing helps you relax and focus.
- Practice the kata slowly before increasing the speed and intensity.
- Visualize your opponent and perform each move with intent and purpose.

- Train with a partner or instructor to receive feedback and improve your technique.

Gankaku Kata is a challenging kata incorporating the movements of a crane to achieve grace, balance, and flow. It is a testament to karate's core principles, including discipline, focus, and precision. Mastering this kata requires patience, dedication, and consistent practice. Whether a beginner or an experienced practitioner, the Gankaku Kata is an excellent addition to your karate training.

Sochin

Sochin floor plan and movements

Sochin Kata, known as "the strength in tranquility," is one of the most prominent katas in karate. Originating from Okinawa, Japan, this kata is practiced by beginner and experienced martial artists due to its benefits for the body and mind. Sochin Kata is a powerful routine requiring focus, flexibility, and discipline. This section dives into the meaning of this kata, its movements, and some tips on how to master it.

Meaning

Sochin Kata is translated as the "tranquil force" or "strength in tranquility." This kata was developed by Chojun Miyagi, the founder of Goju-Ryu Karate, in the early 20th century. The kata combines hard and soft techniques, represented by the smooth and sudden transitions between different stances. The movements in Sochin Kata train the practitioner to become more stable, grounded, and powerful.

Movements

The Sochin Kata consists of 41 movements and is performed at a slow, controlled pace. The kata starts with a slow walking motion, followed by a series of strikes and kicks. The movements within Sochin Kata are done in a fighting stance while breathing in specific patterns. These movements are not only for physical training but also for the mind to focus on the techniques. Sochin Kata emphasizes strong, stable standing postures with wide-stance blocks and low kicks. The kata is performed slowly and deliberately to build concentration and discipline.

Tips

To perform Sochin Kata well, you must master breathing techniques and physical movements. As you exhale during the kata, let out a robust and forceful breath to enhance your power in each movement. Focusing on your technique and form is essential to ensure each movement is precise and accurate. Take time with each motion and practice until it feels comfortable. Then move on to the next movement. Practice the kata in front of a mirror to observe your technique and identify areas to improve.

Sochin Kata is a powerful karate kata to help you develop mindfulness, discipline, and stability. The slow and deliberate movements of the kata allow you to focus on your technique and breathing and strengthen your mind, body, and spirit. Sochin Kata is an impressive routine and a discipline to help you become a better martial artist. With consistent practice, focus, and discipline, you can accomplish greatness and fully embody the strength within tranquility.

Conquering the First Rank of Black Belt

Embarking on the journey to become a black belt in martial arts is no easy feat. It requires dedication, discipline, and perseverance. However, the sense of achievement and pride in earning that first rank is immeasurable. You must master 26 katas, each with unique techniques and movements, to reach this milestone. The glossary of terms at the end of this guide contains all the names and information about these katas, so you can research them further.

You can achieve your black belt through consistent practice and dedication and further your martial arts journey. This chapter discussed the three black belt katas: Kanku-sho, Hangetsu, and Sochin. By studying the fundamentals of these forms, analyzing the techniques, and mastering the proper movements, you will reach your goal of becoming a black belt. The journey is challenging, but the rewards are worth it. Now that you better understand these katas, you can practice and master them.

The following chapters of this book will guide you through the defense techniques, training drills, and dojo etiquette to become a karate master. It might seem daunting, but with the right mindset and guidance, you can conquer each and prove that you can achieve greatness. Imagine the satisfaction when you finally earn that coveted black belt and the sense of accomplishment that comes with it. So, keep practicing, and soon enough, you'll wear a black belt with immense pride.

Chapter 10: Understanding Belts and the Dojo

Understanding the intricacies of the old traditions and customs is essential to mastering the art of karate. The system of ranks in karate is based on colored belts; each color represents your skill level. As you progress in your training, you earn the right to wear a higher belt. But it's not only about the belt. It's about the journey. The dojo, or training hall, is a place where you can physically and mentally push yourself to new limits. It's where you learn discipline, respect, and humility and form bonds with other practitioners sharing your passion.

By understanding the nuances of karate belts and the dojo, you fully immerse yourself in the art and unlock its true power. This chapter closely examines the ten kyus and dan ranking system, titles in karate, and etiquette involved, and teaches you how to tie a belt. The journey of karate starts when you enter the dojo. So, let's begin.

Entering the Dojo

Are you considering joining a martial arts class to improve your physical and mental well-being? Look no further. Karate could be precisely what you need. This ancient Japanese martial art form fosters discipline, focus, and respect for self and others. Whether you want to improve your self-defense skills or experience the physical and mental benefits of training, karate might be the perfect activity. Read on to discover more about this great art form and why you should consider joining a karate dojo today.

The Physical Benefits of Karate

Karate improves balance, coordination, and flexibility. In addition, the nature of the movements and strikes practiced in karate helps develop a lean and agile body over time. As a result, regular karate training leads to a more robust and healthier body. Moreover, practicing karate reduces stress, as the focus required to perform the movements and techniques helps individuals clear their minds of negative thoughts and emotions.

Another reason to consider joining a karate dojo is the community aspect. A karate dojo is a welcoming space for individuals of all ages. It is a place to make friends, cross paths with people from various walks of life, socialize, and have fun. Moreover, practicing karate with people striving toward the same goals can be incredibly motivating and uplifting.

Tips

You must consider a few things when joining a dojo. First, it is crucial to choose the right dojo. Ensure the instructors are certified, experienced, and from a reputable dojo. Take time to observe a class or two before committing to a long-term membership. It is worth checking out reviews from previous or current members, the facilities, and the safety measures in place. As for the training, remember, karate calls for a certain level of respect and discipline. Arriving on time, performing the movements correctly, and being mindful of the other practitioners in the dojo is essential.

Dojo and Sparring Etiquette

Etiquette is taken very seriously in most dojos and is the foundation for a student's training. Part of the training includes sparring, which can be an intimidating experience for those new to the sport. This section discusses the dojo and sparring etiquette expected of beginners and advanced karate practitioners. By following these guidelines, you show respect to your fellow karatekas and become a better martial artist.

Bowing

The first thing you will notice when entering the dojo is everyone bows when they enter and leave the room. Bowing is a sign of respect and should be taken very seriously. Bowing to your training partner before and after each sparring session is an expected and accepted practice. Remember, while sparring, your partner is not your opponent but your training partner. Bowing shows you respect them and their abilities.

Dress Code

Wearing the appropriate attire is expected in the dojo. It includes the karate gi, or uniform, which should be cleaned and ironed before each training session. Long hair should be tied back, and jewelry should not be worn. Showing up dressed inappropriately shows a lack of respect for the art and your fellow karatekas.

Sparring Rules

Before sparring, ask your partner if they are ready to begin. You should also never strike someone who is not mentally or physically prepared. Strikes should be kept light enough to avoid injuring your partner, and any contact in the face or groin is strictly prohibited. Lastly, once a sparring session ends, thank your partner and bow to them as a sign of respect.

Respect for the Teacher

In the dojo, your teacher must be respected and looked up to. You should bow to them as a sign of respect and listen attentively to their instructions. When sparring, obey their commands and never argue. Remember, your teacher is there to help you learn and grow.

Respect for the Dojo

The dojo is a sacred place where students come to train and better themselves. Therefore, it must be treated with respect. Do not eat, drink, or chew gum in the dojo, and keep noise levels to a minimum. Clean up after yourself, and always keep equipment from lying around. By respecting the dojo, you are respecting the art of karate. A karateka must always strive to be humble and respectful, even when competing in tournaments. It gives a better impression of the art.

Understanding Japanese Words in Karate Training

Japanese words are infused into the art form. Knowing them is essential since they are used throughout karate training. This section unlocks the secrets of karate by deciphering Japanese words used in karate training so that you can confidently approach your practice.

- **Sensei:** Sensei means "teacher" in Japanese. This term shows respect to the teacher, who is seen as a mentor and guide. Therefore, correctly addressing your sensei is a sign of respect and an essential aspect of martial arts training.
- **Obi:** An obi is a wide belt worn around the waist with a karate gi. It represents rank and progression in the art, with different color belts representing different levels of achievement in the practice.
- **Shihan:** A Shihan is a master of a martial art. This is the highest title anyone can achieve in karate and requires many years of dedication and commitment to the art.
- **Reigi:** Reigi is the Japanese term for etiquette. Respectful behavior and manners are essential in karate and should always be observed when training and in the dojo.
- **Sempai:** A sempai is a senior to the Kohai or junior students. The sempai must show respect to their teacher and senior students. They often help Kohai understand the techniques taught.
- **Rei:** Rei translates to "respect.". It is the act of bowing in karate, which is a sign of respect and gratitude. It should be done before and after training and when greeting someone at the dojo.

Earning Belts in Karate

TAK Belt Ranking System

Color Belt	Black Belt
Yellow Belt	1ST DAN Black
Orange Belt	2ND DAN Black
Purple Belt	3RD DAN Black
Blue Belt	4TH DAN Black
ADV. Blue Belt	5TH DAN Black
Green Belt	6TH DAN Black
ADV. Green Belt	7TH DAN Black
Brown Belt	8TH DAN Black
INT. Brown Belt	9TH DAN Black
ADV. Brown Belt	10TH DAN Black
Master Brown	

Karate belt ranking system.

One of the most iconic aspects of karate is how students earn belts signifying their proficiency and dedication. In addition, the colorful progression from white to black belts symbolizes hard work, perseverance, and respect toward self and others. This section explores the journey to earning belts in karate and what it entails for students and instructors.

The Basics

Before students can earn belts in karate, they must master the basics of the art, including learning proper stances, footwork, strikes, blocks, and kicks. Basics are the foundation upon which all advanced techniques are built. With a strong foundation, students can progress. Therefore, instructors pay close attention to how students perform the basics, reflecting their discipline and commitment to the art. Students who take shortcuts or neglect basics will need help earning belts in karate.

The Journey of a Beginner

As a beginner in karate, the journey to earning belts often seems daunting. However, acknowledging the progress made at each step is essential. Beginners start with a white belt and must earn their way up the ranks through consistent practice, dedication, and hard work. The first belt is often the hardest to earn, as it sets the tone for the rest of the journey. Instructors work closely with beginners, offering guidance and encouragement to help them overcome challenges and improve their skills.

The Significance of Belt Colors

Each belt color in karate has a specific meaning and significance. For example, the yellow belt represents the sun rising and the beginning of a new day in the journey toward mastery. The green belt represents a growing plant, signifying growth and progress. As students advance through the belt ranks, they better understand the art and its principles. Belt tests involve proficiency in techniques and katas, etiquette, and respect toward instructors and fellow students.

The Role of Competition

While earning belts in karate isn't about winning competitions, competition is significant in the journey toward mastery. Competitions allow students to test their skills against others and gain experience in a controlled environment. Winning competitions isn't the goal; it's learning from the experience and improving skills. Instructors often encourage students to participate in competitions to help them grow in their understanding of karate and themselves.

The Rewards of Earning a Black Belt

The ultimate goal for many karate students is to earn a black belt, which signifies mastery of the art. Earning a black belt is a significant achievement representing years of dedication and hard work. More than just a physical symbol, a black belt means a mindset of humility, respect, and continuous learning. Students who earn a black belt often find the journey more rewarding than the destination, as they have grown in all aspects of their lives.

The 10 Kyu and Dan Ranking System

One essential aspect of karate is the ranking system outlining a student's progress and skills. The ranking system is known as the 10 Kyu and Dan systems, used worldwide by karate schools and organizations. This section details the 10 Kyu and Dan ranking system, the different ranks' meanings, and how to progress through the levels.

The 10 Kyu and Dan ranking systems are used to grade students' skills and knowledge of karate. The system comprises ten Kyu ranks, from the lowest to the highest. Colored belts represent the Kyu ranks, and each rank has its own set of skills and techniques. For example, the lowest rank is the white belt, followed by the yellow, orange, green, blue, purple, and belts. The different ranks represent the various stages of learning, with each color representing a proficiency level.

After the Kyu ranks, the Dan ranks. These are the black belt ranks and are divided into ten degrees. The first-degree black belt is Shodan. The highest rank is the tenth degree, awarded to masters. The Dan ranks signify a level of mastery and are a symbol of excellence in karate. Dan ranks are usually awarded after several years of practice and dedication. Achieving a black belt is no easy feat, requiring hard work, discipline, and perseverance.

One way to progress in the ranking system is by regularly attending karate classes. Consistent practice and training are essential to advance through the ranks. Many schools have a minimum waiting period for progression between ranks, usually three to six months. It ensures students have enough time to master the skills and knowledge required for the next level.

Karate students must take an exam to move up the ranks. Students are tested on their techniques, knowledge of karate, and physical ability. The exam is usually conducted by a panel of black belt instructors who grade the students' performance. The exam can include kata tests, a prearranged sequence of movements, sparring, and breaking boards.

Karate Titles

Karate is one of the oldest martial arts in the world and is practiced by millions of people globally. But did you know that karate comes with a unique system of titles? These titles signify the level of expertise and proficiency practitioners have achieved. This section looks at the different karate titles and their meanings. So, buckle up, and delve into the fascinating world of karate titles.

The Beginner Titles

In karate, the beginner rank is known as the Kyu rank. Usually, practitioners start at the 10th rank and progress from there. The Kyu ranks are numbered, beginning with ten and descending toward one. Any student below the Kyu rank is considered a novice. The Kyu rank titles are usually colored belts denoting the student's expertise level. For example, a yellow belt signifies a fifth Kyu rank, while a blue belt is the third Kyu rank.

The Dan Titles

After advancing through the Kyu ranks, a student progresses to a Dan rank. The Dan ranks begin from the first Dan, signifying the first-degree black belt. Dan ranks go up to the tenth Dan, the highest level in karate. The Dan titles are usually awarded based on the student's mastery of various karate techniques, performance during tournaments, and contribution to the karate community.

The Master Titles

The master titles are usually awarded to the highest-ranking karate practitioners. These titles include Renshi, Shihan, Kyoshi, and Hanshi. These titles are earned through decades of mastering different karate forms and techniques. A Renshi usually refers to a teacher who has completed their fifth Dan. A Shihan denotes a teacher who has met their eighth Dan and shown excellent teaching skills.

The Reference Titles

Besides the Kyu, Dan, and Master titles, karate has many reference titles denoting a person's contribution to karate. Some of these titles include Soke, Kokusai Budoin, and Kaiso. A Soke is a person who founded a particular karate style and is regarded as its father. The Kokusai Budoin is an organization recognizing outstanding karate practitioners worldwide.

The Ceremony of Awarding Titles

Awarding titles is considered the highest mark of honor in the karate community. During the ceremony, the practitioner is awarded their new title, and their achievements are recognized. The ceremony is usually attended by other karate students who have attained similar titles.

Step-By-Step Tutorial on How to Tie a Belt

If you're new to karate, one of the first things you must learn is how to tie your belt. Not only is it an essential part of your uniform, but also a symbol of your progress and dedication to the martial art. It might seem tricky the first time you attempt to tie your belt, but it becomes second nature with practice. This step-by-step tutorial walks you through the process so you can tie your belt like a pro.

- **Step 1:** Place the center of the belt on your navel and wrap it around your waist. Make sure you have equal length on both sides.
- **Step 2:** Cross the ends over each other at the back and bring them to the front again.
- **Step 3:** Take the right end of the belt and tuck it under both layers. Pull it up and over the left end of the belt. Next, take the left end of the belt and tuck it under the right end and through the loop you've just created. Pull both ends of the belt tight to secure the knot.
- **Step 4:** Adjust the belt by pulling the ends to make it comfortable. Ensure the belt is even around your waist and the knot is centered on your body.
- **Step 5:** Tuck any loose ends of the belt into the folds at your waist. Stand tall, proud, and ready to start your karate training.

Learning to tie your karate belt might be confusing at first, but if you follow the steps above, you'll have it down in no time. Remember, your belt is not just a piece of clothing but an important symbol of your karate journey. Therefore, always treat it with respect and care. Practice tying your belt before class so you don't feel rushed or pressured before practice.

Belts and ranks are not just symbolic in karate. They represent your skills, progress, and accomplishments. From the beginner's level, the ten kyus, to the advanced level, the dan ranking system, every level is challenging and rewarding. Remember the karate titles that inspire practitioners to become better martial artists, such as Sensei, Shihan, and Hanshi. Respect for the dojo, your instructor, and fellow students is crucial. Also, proper sparring etiquette and simple Japanese words like "oss" and "rei" will enhance your training experience.

Chapter 11: How to Defend Yourself with Karate

Learning karate is not only about mastering a new skill. It's about gaining confidence to defend yourself in any situation. Whether walking home late at night or confronting a bully, knowing how to protect yourself with karate can make all the difference. With its focus on discipline, fitness, and self-defense, karate gives you the tools to protect yourself while improving your overall health and well-being.

Karate can teach you discipline and help you defend yourself.
https://www.pexels.com/photo/woman-wearing-white-karati-g-under-blue-sky-3023756/

This chapter explains why karate is an excellent tool for personal defense. It discusses how Shotokan karate was created as an art of self-defense and offers tips on how to use karate in different situations. Finally, it examines the vital points you should target to defend yourself effectively. Nobody should feel helpless or scared to go out in public. With the proper techniques, karate can give you the confidence and skills to stay safe.

Why Karate Should Be Your Go-To for Self-Defense

Self-defense has become a necessity in today's world. With the increasing number of crimes, protecting self has become a priority. As a result, many martial arts have developed, and choosing the right one for self-defense can be overwhelming. However, karate has stood the test of time and proven an effective tool for defense. This section explores why karate should be your go-to martial art for self-defense.

Karate is an excellent martial art to help you become physically and mentally demanding. It is a physical exercise and focuses on mental discipline. The practice of karate requires dedication and discipline, helping you develop perseverance, strength, and focus. In addition, by practicing karate, you become physically more potent and confident, helping you defend against a potential attacker.

Karate focuses on strikes, kicks, and blocks, making it the perfect martial art for self-defense. These strikes can incapacitate an attacker without causing severe harm. Moreover, karate does not rely on weapons, meaning you can defend yourself in any situation. The blocks and strikes taught in karate can be delivered with speed, power, and precision, neutralizing an attacker effectively.

Karate teaches you to avoid and evade attacks. The best way to prevent an attack is to recognize the danger signs early. Karate teaches you to be aware of your surroundings, identify potential threats, and act quickly. Techniques like body shifting and distancing can create space between you and the attacker, allowing you to defend yourself successfully.

Another benefit of karate is it can be practiced by anyone regardless of age and gender. It is a great way to get fit, stay active, and relieve stress. Learning karate gives you the confidence to protect yourself, your loved ones, and your property. By practicing karate, you learn self-discipline, self-control, and self-awareness, essential skills in any self-defense situation.

Shotokan Karate: An Art of Self-Defense

Learning self-defense has become necessary as violence continues to plague society. Regarding martial arts for self-defense, Shotokan karate should be considered. With its roots in Japan, this martial art provides a comprehensive system of strikes, kicks, blocks, and throws to defend against an attacker. This section delves deeper into the art of Shotokan Karate, explores its history, philosophy, and techniques, and why it's worth pursuing your fitness and self-defense needs.

History and Philosophy

Shotokan karate traces its roots back to Gichin Funakoshi, who developed this art in the early 20th century based on the principles of Okinawa Karate. Funakoshi's goal was to promote physical and mental discipline, character development, and mutual respect through martial arts training. He named his art "Shotokan," meaning "House of Shoto," his pen name. Today, Shotokan karate has become one of the most popular martial arts styles, with millions of practitioners globally. Its primary focus is basic techniques such as punching, kicking, striking, and blocking, designed to build strength, speed, and coordination.

The Techniques of Shotokan Karate

Shotokan karate is known for its powerful and explosive techniques, requiring much focus and precision. The art emphasizes solid stances, proper posture, and effective breathing techniques to generate power and speed. Here are common Shotokan karate techniques you'll learn in a beginner's class:

- **Punches**: There are four basic punches in Shotokan Karate, including the front punch (Jodan Zuki), reverse punch (Gyaku Zuki), uppercut (Chudan Tsuki), and hook punch (Kagi Tsuki).
- **Kicks**: Shotokan karate includes various kicks, including a front kick (Mae Geri), side kick (Yoko Geri), hook kick (Uchi Mikazuki Geri), and spinning kick (Chudan Mawashi Geri).
- **Blocks**: Effective blocking is essential to defend against incoming attacks. The art of Shotokan karate features several blocking techniques, including the high block (Jodan Uke), the

low block (Gedan Barai), the middle block (Chudan Uke), and the inward block (Uchiake).

Benefits of Shotokan Karate

Shotokan karate training offers many benefits beyond self-defense. Here are some benefits you can gain from practicing Shotokan Karate:

- **Improved Physical Fitness:** Shotokan karate provides a comprehensive workout improving cardiovascular health, increasing strength and flexibility, and enhancing balance and coordination.
- **Boosted Confidence:** As you progress in your Shotokan karate training, you gain confidence in your abilities, translating into other areas of your life.
- **Self-Discipline:** Shotokan karate requires dedication, commitment, and focus, developing self-discipline and determination.
- **Stress Relief:** The physical and mental exertion involved in Shotokan karate training provides a cathartic release of stress and tension.

Shotokan karate is a holistic practice with numerous benefits to enhance physical and mental well-being. So, whether you want to improve your self-defense skills, build confidence, or boost your fitness level, Shotokan karate is an excellent choice. It's a discipline requiring patience, commitment, and practice, but the payoff is well worth it.

Performing karate Maneuvers against Unarmed Offenders

Do you get worried when walking home alone at night? Or do you have to walk through a bad neighborhood to get where you're going? If so, it's essential to know some self-defense techniques. Karate is one of the most common and effective forms of self-defense. This section covers a few karate maneuvers you can use against unarmed offenders.

- **Palm Heel Strike:** This technique is perfect for striking the nose or chin of an assailant who has grabbed your collar or shoulder. To execute this maneuver, make a fist with your hand and turn it so it's facing inward. Next, forcefully use your palm to strike your opponent's chin or nose. It should cause them to stumble backward, giving you time to escape.
- **Knee Strike:** The knee strike is ideal for an attacker standing before you. To execute this maneuver, bring your knee upward,

and thrust your knee toward your opponent's groin with the toes pointing down. It will provide more than enough time to escape or fight them off.

- **Elbow Strike:** The elbow strike is a great technique when fighting in cramped quarters, like a bar or at home. Throw your elbow directly toward your opponent's jaw to perform this movement. This move can knock an attacker out, giving you enough time to flee.
- **Back Kick:** The back kick is perfect when someone sneaks up on you. To use this technique, bring your foot up behind you, then turn around to kick directly backward. This kick can catch an attacker off balance and send them reeling, giving you enough time to get away.
- **Hammer Fist Strike:** This technique is perfect for striking the back of your opponent's head. To perform a hammer fist strike, form your hand into a fist and strike your opponent's head with the flat part of your hand. This action can cause your opponent to lose consciousness long enough for you to escape.

Knowing basic karate moves can help you feel more confident when walking alone or in an unfamiliar area. You never know when you might need to use a self-defense technique to protect yourself. However, learning these five methods can provide the necessary tools to defend yourself effectively should the need arise. Remember, using self-defense techniques should always be a last resort, and calling for help from the authorities should always be your first action.

Defending Yourself from Armed Assailants

One of the most terrifying situations anyone could find themselves in is a confrontation with an armed assailant. Being a victim of armed assault is something nobody wants to experience. But what if it happens to you? How can you defend yourself and stay safe in such a situation?

- **Be Prepared:** Preparation is vital to any defensive situation. In case of an armed attack, your preparation should include knowing your surroundings and having an exit plan. Remember, every second counts when facing an armed assailant, so it pays to be prepared.
- **Stay Calm:** It is challenging to stay calm in a stressful situation, but it is crucial when facing an armed assailant. The attacker is already in an agitated state of mind, so getting worked up only

escalates the situation. Being calm allows you to think and act rationally, helping you gain control of the problem.
- **Fight Back:** If you are being attacked, and running away is not an option, fighting back might be your only recourse. Knowing basic self-defense techniques like kicks, punches, and blocks can help you fend off the attacker and buy enough time to call for help or wait for the authorities to arrive.
- **Use Available Tools:** In case of an armed attack, any tool can be helpful. For example, items like keys, pepper spray, or a tactical pen can be used to defend yourself. These tools might seem small, but they can cause severe damage to an assailant, allowing you to escape or control the situation.
- **Seek Training:** It is essential to get training to defend yourself in an armed attack. You don't have to be a martial arts expert to defend yourself. However, basic self-defense training like Krav Maga or kickboxing can make a huge difference in a life-or-death situation.

Mastering Karate Moves to Defend against Different Weapon Attacks

Karate is a self-defense martial art useful in various situations, especially when dealing with weapon attacks. Knowing how to defend yourself against knives, bats, or sticks gives you a sense of security and empowerment. Here are some karate moves you can master to protect yourself from weapon attacks.
- **Against Knife Attacks:** To defend against a knife attack, position your hands in front of your face, with one foot back and the other forward. Wait for the attacker to move toward you and use your forearm to block the hand holding the knife. Then, quickly strike their face, neck, or groin with a punch or kick to distract and create an opportunity to disarm them.
- **Against Bat Attacks:** If someone is attacking you with a bat, move to the side to avoid direct impact and use your forearm to block the bat. Then, use your other arm to strike the attacker's neck or face with a punch or elbow strike. You can also kick their knees to destabilize them and create an opening for counterattacks.
- **Against Stick Attacks:** When faced with a stick attack, use your forearm to block the impact and strike the attacker's head,

throat, or chest with a punch or knife-hand strike. If the attacker holds the stick with both hands, you can use a double-forearm block to deflect the attack and then counter with a punch or kick.

- **Against Multiple Weapons:** If the attacker has more than one weapon, you must be aware of all the threats and prioritize your defense. One strategy is to move swiftly and evade the attacks while looking for opportunities to disarm the attacker. Another approach is to defend against one weapon at a time and neutralize the attacker's balance and stance.

- **Against Surprise Attacks:** In case of a surprise attack, your reaction time and awareness are crucial. Maintain a relaxed but alert posture and use your peripheral vision to detect signs of danger. If you sense an attack, quickly move to the side, and use a combination of blocks and strikes to create space and time to react.

Karate moves can be a valuable tool in personal defense against various weapon attacks. However, mastering these moves requires practice, dedication, and the guidance of an experienced instructor. Remember, the best defense is to avoid dangerous situations and seek help from law enforcement or other authorities when facing threats. So, stay safe, and keep practicing.

Chapter 12: Daily Training Drills

Engaging in a karate training regimen can be one of the most significant decisions you'll ever make. It promotes physical fitness and cultivates mental and emotional wellness. Regular exercise can reduce stress and anxiety, improve focus and cognitive function, and alleviate symptoms of depression. But what sets karate apart from other exercises is its required discipline and dedication. As a result, you'll improve your physical prowess and acquire valuable life skills, such as patience, self-control, and perseverance.

This chapter outlines a daily karate training regimen you can follow at the gym or in the comfort of your home. It breaks down several drills and routines to enhance physical fitness, agility, speed, and power. The exercises cater to beginners and can be adapted for advanced practitioners.

Exercise can help you progress in karate.
https://www.pexels.com/photo/man-running-on-sand-field-2827392/

Warm-Up Exercises

Karate involves many high-impact movements, so a proper warm-up routine is crucial to avoid injury. A good warm-up should include cardio to raise your heart rate and stretching exercises to prepare your muscles and joints. Recommended warm-up exercises include jumping jacks, skipping rope, leg swings, and hip rotations.

Kicking and Punching Drills

Karate is all about mastering the various kicks and punches. Practicing them repeatedly, alone and with partners, is essential to perfect these moves. Training equipment like punching bags and kick pads can add resistance and intensity to your drills. Continuous practice builds muscle memory, leading to automatic movements and better overall technique.

Muscle Conditioning Exercises

Karate requires solid and powerful muscles to execute moves with speed and precision. Incorporating exercises like squats, lunges, and push-ups into your training regimen builds strength and endurance. These exercises strengthen the core muscles, which are essential for balance and stability. Using weighted bars or kettlebells can help you take your muscle conditioning routine to the next level.

Plyometric Training

Plyometric training is a specific workout to improve explosive power. In karate, this translates to higher jumps, faster kicks, and more decisive and quick strikes. Plyometric exercises include jump squats, burpees, and box jumps, focusing on rapidly contracting and extending the muscles. When done correctly, plyometrics can significantly improve physical performance. However, executing the exercises flawlessly and taking time with them is critical.

Resistance Band Exercises

Resistant band exercises are excellent for training the weaker muscle groups and preparing the body for high-impact moves. Focusing on specific muscle groups most used in karate training wraps up a comprehensive workout regimen. The resistance of the bands helps build strength, endurance, and flexibility.

Cardiovascular Training

Karate emphasizes overall fitness and health, including a solid cardiovascular system. Combining aerobic exercises, such as running or cycling, with anaerobic exercises, like jumping or sprinting, provides an effective training regimen that strengthens the heart and improves stamina. A good mix of high- and low-intensity exercises is ideal for a well-rounded workout. For example, complete a 30-minute cardio session at least twice weekly to boost endurance and cardiovascular health.

Stability and Core Training

Exercises focusing on promoting balance, stability, and coordination help execute various karate positions efficiently. These exercises include planks, mountain climbers, and single-leg balance exercises strengthening the muscles around the hips, lower body, and spine. While not directly related to martial arts, squats and deadlifts also strengthen core muscles. The core is essential for balance and stability in all martial arts, so incorporate these exercises into your routine.

Cool-Down Exercises

After completing a strenuous karate workout, it is essential to cool down properly to prevent muscle soreness and injury. Stretching exercises and slow cardio activities like jogging or walking reduce the heart rate gradually and aids in better blood circulation to the muscles, helping with muscle recovery. Take time to stretch after each workout to improve flexibility and prevent muscle tightness. If you feel incredibly sore after a session, taking an ice bath or using a cold compress can do wonders for keeping muscle inflammation at bay.

Meditation

Taking time off your busy schedule to relax and focus on breathing can improve concentration, reduce stress, and boost overall well-being. Use meditation to visualize certain moves or techniques to help you understand them better. There are many ways to meditate, so feel free to experiment and find the one that suits you best. Even a few minutes of dedicated meditation can help you stay focused and motivated while training.

Weekly Routine

Now that you know the basics, it's time to create a routine. Aim for 3-4 days of karate training a week, depending on your skill level and fitness goals. Supplement your training with other exercises, like running or swimming, for a complete workout. Ensure each session involves warm-up, plyometric exercises, resistance band exercises, cardio training, stability or core training, and cool-down exercises. It's important to incorporate rest and meditation days into your routine. Your body needs time to recover after a strenuous workout, so take at least one day off a week to allow your muscles to heal and prevent injury.

- **Monday:** Cardio Training – 30 minutes
- **Tuesday:** Plyometric Exercises – 20 minutes
- **Wednesday:** Rest and Meditation
- **Thursday:** Resistance Band Exercises – 25 minutes
- **Friday:** Core and Stability Training – 20 minutes
- **Saturday:** karate Drills – 40 minutes
- **Sunday:** Stretching and Cool-Down Exercises – 20 minutes

This routine will help you stay in shape, improve your technique, and increase your karate skills. However, everyone is different, so feel free to experiment with other exercises and routines until you find the one that works best.

A comprehensive karate training regimen helps you achieve your goals by focusing on your physical and mental well-being. A thorough karate workout that includes warm-up exercises, kicking and punching drills, muscle conditioning exercises, plyometric training, resistance band exercises, cardiovascular training, stability, core exercises, and cool-down exercises will pave your path to karate success. In addition, regular training, dedication, discipline in following your karate goals, and consistent practice with commitment result in achieving your karate goals and a well-balanced diet with proper nutrition. So, go ahead, build your regimen, and achieve excellence in karate.

Extra: Pressure Points Overview and Karate Terms

Whether a seasoned practitioner or just starting, understanding pressure points is crucial for mastering the art of karate. By targeting these specific areas of the body, you can quickly disable an opponent and gain the upper hand in a fight. Since karate has a unique vocabulary, this final chapter explores popular terms you should be familiar with. So, get ready to kick, punch, and chop your way to success.

Striking Points and Their Locations

In self-defense, knowing which vital striking points can take someone down is essential, especially if you're physically more petite than your attacker. Striking points are pressure points throughout the body that can cause pain, imbalance, and even unconsciousness. Here are some points to consider:

- **Temple Point:** One of the most common striking points is the temple. By striking the temple point on both sides of the head, near the hairline, you can cause a sudden shock to the brain, resulting in disorientation and confusion. It gives you time to react and defend yourself against the attacker.
- **Jawline Point:** Another crucial striking point is the jawline point below the ear. When struck correctly, it causes intense pain, disorientation, and damage to the attacker's inner ear, resulting in imbalance. On the other hand, a strong punch or elbow

strike to this point can immobilize the attacker temporarily, giving you time to flee.
- **Collarbone Point:** The collarbone point is at the lower edge of the front of the collarbone. Striking this point can cause extreme pain and discomfort, leading to temporary paralysis and difficulty breathing. However, striking this point can buy you a few seconds to escape if you're being attacked from the front.
- **Solar Plexus Point:** The solar plexus point is in the center of the torso, just below the ribcage. Striking this point can cause a sudden loss of breath, resulting in temporary paralysis and even unconsciousness. However, punches, kicks, or even a quick jab to this point can be highly effective in stopping an attacker.
- **Groin Point:** The groin point is between the legs, below the beltline. Striking this point will cause intense pain, especially in males, resulting in temporary paralysis and disorientation. While not guaranteed to stop an attacker, it can give you time to escape or bring them to the ground.

Karate Terminology

Now that you know the essential striking points, it's time to learn the basics of karate terminology. Here are terms and phrases you should be familiar with:

26 Katas
1. Heian Shodan
2. Heian Nidan
3. Heian Sandan
4. Heian Yondan
5. Heian Godan
6. Tekki Shodan
7. Tekki Nidan
8. Tekki Sandan
9. Bassai Dai
10. Bassai Sho
11. Kanku Dai

12. Kanku Sho
13. Empi
14. Hangetsu
15. Jion
16. Jiin
17. Wankan
18. Meikyo
19. Unsu
20. Sochin
21. Nijushiho
22. Gojushiho-Te
23. Chinte
24. Jitte
25. Gankaku
26. Gojushho-Dai

Japanese Numbers
1. Ichi
2. Ni
3. San
4. Shi/Yon
5. Go
6. Roku
7. Shichi/Nana
8. Hachi
9. Ku/Kyuu
10. Juu

Karate Stances
- Zenkutsu-Dachi (Forward Stance)
- Kiba-Dachi (Horse Stance)
- Heiko-Dachi (Parallel Stance)
- Shiko-Dachi (Sumo Stance)
- Tsuru-Ashi-Dachi (Crane Stance)

- Neko-Ashi-Dachi (Cat Stance)
- Kokutsu-Dachi (Back Stance)
- Hangetsu-Dachi (Half Moon Stance)

Karate Techniques
- Uke (block)
- Tsuki (punching)
- Uchi (striking)
- Geri (kicking)
- Kihon (foundational training)
- Kata (form or pattern)
- Kumite (sparring)
- Tanden (center of gravity)
- Goshin-Jitsu (self-defense)
- Shime-Waza (grappling techniques)
- Atemi-Waza (vital point striking)
- Kime (focus)
- Jiyu-Kumite (free sparring)
- Ukemi (break-falling)
- Ikken Hisatsu (one-strike kill)
- Kyusho-Jitsu (vital point striking)

Now that you know the essential striking points, stances, and techniques of karate, it's time to start practicing. Find karate classes near you and start training with an experienced teacher. With practice and dedication, you'll master the art of karate and become a proficient fighter.

Conclusion

Karate is an ancient martial art practiced for centuries, originating in Okinawa, Japan. It is a highly disciplined form of self-defense focusing on physical and mental training to develop the mind and body. This martial art is about punches and kicks and developing a strong mindset, discipline, respect, and humility. This ultimate guide covered everything from the basics to the advanced techniques of karate.

The karate mindset is one of the most critical aspects of this martial art. karate teaches you how to be disciplined, focused, and mentally strong. It's a way of life requiring respect for yourself and others. You must be committed to your practice and persevere through challenging situations to develop this mindset. Also, aim to be humble with a positive attitude. Meditation and visualization exercises are essential to developing the karate mindset.

Kihon is the foundational training of karate and includes basic stances and blocks. These techniques are the building blocks for more advanced techniques. This guide taught you basic postures, like the front, back, and horse stances. You learned the basic blocks, such as the inward, outward, and rising blocks. These techniques are crucial for defense and are used in conjunction with strikes. This book covered proper punching techniques, such as the straight punch, hook punch, and uppercut, and explored various kicks, including the front, roundhouse, and sidekicks. Proper form and technique are essential for effective strikes.

Katas are prearranged sequences of movements simulating a real fight. Kumite, or sparring, is another essential component of karate training. This comprehensive guide covered the katas and kumite techniques for each belt level. You learned to perform the katas correctly, the importance of proper technique, and how to apply your techniques in kumite to defend yourself against opponents. In addition, this book provided a guide to understanding belts and the Dojo culture. It discussed the different belt levels, what they represent, and the etiquette expected within the Dojo environment.

This guide provided an overview of pressure points and a glossary of terms. Knowing the body's pressure points can immobilize your opponent and control the situation. Understanding karate terminology is essential for proper communication within the Dojo. At the end of this book, you should have a solid understanding of the basics, skills, and knowledge to take your karate training to the next level. With consistent practice and dedication, you can master the art of karate and develop a powerful mindset to serve you well in defending yourself.

From the foundational stances and blocks to the advanced black belt katas and self-defense techniques, karate provides physical and mental training for individuals of all ages and backgrounds. With consistent practice and training, you can improve your skills, develop a strong mindset, and achieve your karate goals. Additionally, check the glossary of terms at the end of this guide to refresh your knowledge and enhance your karate journey. Good luck, and happy training.

Here's another book by Clint Sharp that you might like

CLINT SHARP

Muay Thai

A COMPREHENSIVE GUIDE TO THAI BOXING BASICS FOR BEGINNERS AND A COMPARISON WITH DUTCH KICKBOXING

References

Chen, S. (2021, January 30). 14 basic karate stances help you build a strong base. The karate Blog. https://thekarateblog.com/karate-stances/

Grupp, J. (2003). Shotokan karate Kata: Volume 2 (1st ed.). Meyer & Meyer Sport. https://www.shotokankaratecalgary.com/kata.php

Jutras, M., & The karate Lifestyle. (n.d.). The complete list of basic karate stances. Thekaratelifestyle.com. https://www.thekaratelifestyle.com/list-of-karate-stances/

Karate - Belt Colours & Meaning. (n.d.). Tutorialspoint.com. https://www.tutorialspoint.com/karate/karate_belt_colours_meaning.htm

Karate belts. (2015, June 11). Elite Martial Arts Karate Dojo. https://emadojola.com/karate-belts/

Koch, C. (2023, January 1). karate Kata list of 10 different karate styles [2023]. The karate Blog. https://thekarateblog.com/karate-kata-list/

List of Shotokan katas (with video & written instructions). (2018, September 7). Black Belt Wiki. https://blackbeltwiki.com/shotokan-karate-katas

Shotokan katas. (n.d.). Victoria Shotokan karate and Kobudo Association. https://www.shotokankarate.ca/katas

Vladisavljevic, V. (2022, July 19). Karate belt order: Ranking system explained. Way of Martial Arts. https://wayofmartialarts.com/karate-belts-ranking-system-explained/

Printed in Great Britain
by Amazon